LOVE
MADE
PERFECT

LOVE
MADE
PERFECT
Foundations for the Holy Life

WILLIAM M. GREATHOUSE

Beacon Hill Press of Kansas City
Kansas City, Missouri

Copyright 1997
by Beacon Hill Press of Kansas City

ISBN 083-411-6545
Continuing Lay Training Unit 115.25a
Printed in the
United States of America

Cover Design: Kevin Williamson

"Light for Your Spiritual Journey" sections: Wesley Tracy

Library of Congress Cataloging-in-Publication Data
Greathouse, William M.
    Love made perfect : foundations for the holy life / William M.
    Greathouse.
        p.   cm.
    ISBN 0-8341-1654-5 (pbk.)
    1. Sanctification. 2. Perfection—Religious aspects—Christianity.
3. Theology, Doctrinal. 4. Christian life—Nazarene authors.   I. Title.
BT766.G73   1997
248.4—dc21   97-34246
                                                                         CIP

10   9   8   7   6   5   4   3   2   1

To my three children,
Becky, Mark, and Beth,
"who walk in the truth,"
and to
Ruth,
who has shared my ministry
for more than half a century.

Contents

Foreword

"I have sensed a special closeness to God as I have written," said William Greathouse in a letter to me that accompanied the final chapters of this book. He added, "Yet now it seems so earthy, so human."

I think that may be the strength of this book—profound scholarship baptized with devotion, plus the human touch. In this book Dr. Greathouse does not merely teach *about* holiness; he *teaches* holiness. The difference is the difference between an outside scientist taking down observation notes and an insider, a participant, sharing knowledge, insights, and wisdom.

In a valedictory article in the *Herald of Holiness* upon his retirement as a general superintendent in the Church of the Nazarene, Dr. Greathouse wrote, "The message of holiness remains for me the essence of the gospel—God's pure love reigning in the heart and excluding sin. This experience is both the command of the law and the promise of the gospel. To the proclamation and exposition of this message I have dedicated my life."[1]

This book shows that though he retired from official leadership in 1989, he has not retired from the proclamation and exposition of the message to which he has dedicated his life. No preacher or teacher of my denomination has during my lifetime made the doctrine of entire sanctification as clear, as sensible, and as desirable as has William Greathouse.

I used to teach a course at Nazarene Theological Seminary called Homiletical Study of Holiness. Each term I would tell my students that there were three great preachers who during my lifetime successfully preached holiness across denominational lines like world citizens: D. Elton Trueblood, E. Stanley Jones, and Paul S. Rees. They preached holiness to any audience, liberal or conservative, Protestant or Catholic. They could do this, I told my students, because they avoided sectarian, red-flag rhetoric in favor of biblical language. Letting the Bible speak for itself, they did not win any sectarian wars—but they did get people to open their hearts to the Spirit of God. I would ask my students what they wanted to accomplish as preachers of scriptural holiness—did they want to win a hairsplitting debate, or would they rather get believers to open their hearts to all God has for them and to commit themselves to Christlikeness?

If I ever teach such a course again, I will add the name Bill Greathouse to the world-class list of holiness teachers and preachers. In a real sense, Bill Greathouse is a child of the Church of the Nazarene. In the *Herald of Holiness* article quoted above, he urged Nazarenes to continue to "teach and preach Christian perfection as (1) a doctrine to be believed, (2) an experience to be received, (3) a life to be lived, and (4) a discipline to be enforced."[2] As you will see in this book, his teaching is distinctively Wesleyan. But far beyond, and more important than denominational or ideological loyalty, is the fact that Dr. Greathouse's message in this book is thoroughly and soundly biblical. He lets the Bible speak for itself.

Thus, in every Christian tradition that honors the Bible as the Rule for faith and practice, Dr. Greathouse will be a welcomed guest. The message of Christian holiness is broader than sectarian boundaries and deeper than ideological debates. Therefore, whatever your background or denominational preference, this book is for you if you

hunger to know more of God,

long to find sanctifying grace,

want to understand scriptural holiness,

wonder whether or not Christian holiness is truly
    a Bible doctrine,

are searching for the fullness of the Spirit,

always thought you could never be free from the
    inward sin that bedevils your best efforts at
    discipleship,

in your best moments thirst to be more Christlike.

If nothing in the foregoing list applies to you, then you might as well reach for the remote control now.

At Dr. Greathouse's request, I have prepared spiritual formation exercises at the end of each chapter. Carrying out the theme of "Foundations for the Holy Life," I have used this format: Cornerstones, Spiritual Stepping-stones, and Tools to Work With. Primarily, though not exclusively, the Cornerstones section provides ways to review, analyze, and evaluate the content of the chapter (the cognitive objective). The Spiritual Stepping-stones activities primarily explore the affective domain. They are aimed at helping the student process issues of the heart such as feelings, appreciations, and values. Though the cognitive and affective activities are usually expressed in behavioral terms, the Tools to Work With section at the end of each chapter usually presents instruments and assignments of things to *use* and *do* (the psychomotor objective). The exercise for chapter 10 is different from the others, being a seeker's guide to receiving sanctifying grace.

—WESLEY D. TRACY
Editor, "Herald of Holiness"

Acknowledgements

Credit for this book goes largely to my friend Wesley Tracy, without whom it would not have been born. As editor of the *Herald of Holiness* Dr. Tracy requested that I write a series of articles on Christian holiness for the publication. These pieces form the nucleus of this little volume. Wes then graciously consented to provide the helpful spiritual formation exercises at the close of each chapter. These exercises are designed not only to facilitate a clearer cognitive grasp of the truth presented in each chapter but also to guide the reader in processing that truth in experience and life.

The final form of this book owes much to the faithful editorial work of my daughter-in-law Jan Greathouse (an English composition teacher with few peers). Jan has not only eliminated some of my stylistic infelicities but also by her spiritual insights often helped me say more clearly what I intended to convey. Like my children, Jan, too, "walks in the truth."

Thanks are also due to Shona Fisher and Bonnie Perry who edited the manuscript as well as to Kelly Gallagher and Paul Martin who have shepherded the project through to completion.

Finally, I am indebted to David Felter, director of Christian Lay Training, and his committee, for choosing *Love Made Perfect* as the denominational study book for 1998.

William M. Greathouse
Trevecca Nazarene University
Nashville, Tennessee

So that you may love him with all your heart
and with all your soul, and live.

—Deut. 30:6, NIV

1

The Promise
of Perfect Love

WHAT THE WORLD NEEDS NOW IS LOVE, SWEET love," a once-popular song says, echoing a truism of current culture. The song is right to a certain extent. We do need love, but not the love that pop singers twang their guitars about. We need the love the Bible speaks of—*perfect* love. How we hunger for God's perfect love to fill our hearts, expelling everything contrary to love and reproducing Christ in us (1 John 4:17)!

Is such love something we can only dream about? Not if we believe the gospel. The promise of the gospel is that we can receive and manifest perfect love.

English reformer John Wesley (1703-91) recovered for the Church this scriptural truth that had been shoved into the background in much of Protestant practice.

In one form or another, the doctrine of Christian perfection—understood as a realizable experience of heart purity and perfect love leading to a life of Christlikeness—had lain at the heart of the Christian tradition from the time of Jesus and the apostles and found expression in both Eastern Orthodoxy and Roman Catholicism.

Then came the Reformation, with a rediscovery of the truth of salvation by faith. Particularly in the case of Martin Luther (1483-1546), this rediscovery of justification by faith produced an overreaction against the church's teaching on holiness. In his zeal to avoid anything that smacked of salvation by works (the Roman Catholic pursuit of holiness Luther had tried and found wanting), Martin neglected too much the "Be ye holy; for I am holy" of the Bible (1 Pet. 1:16, KJV).

"Right here Wesley rose to mountain heights," claims the late George Croft Cell of Boston University. "He restored the neglected doctrine of holiness to its merited position in the Protestant understanding of Christianity."[1]

The Neglected Doctrine

It is critically important that we see with clarity the *essence* of this "neglected doctrine of holiness," the doctrine of Christian perfection seen as perfect love.

The Bible word translated *perfect* means "end" or "intended purpose."

The New Testament word for *perfection* is not a static but a dynamic, functional term. Our English word comes from the Latin *perfectio,* which means "absolute perfection" or "sinlessness." The New Testament word, the Greek *teleios,* derives from the root *telos,* which means "end" or "intended purpose." A thing is "perfect" when it answers to its true end. For example, the pen now in my hand is perfect, not because it is flawless, but because it writes. It answers to the end for which it was designed.

Deploring the connotation of the English word *perfect,*

Wesley nevertheless refused to give up his doctrine of perfection because, correctly understood, perfection is a scriptural term.

What Wesley did was to *redefine* perfection according to its New Testament meaning. Adam Clarke summarized the Wesleyan and New Testament idea of perfection when he explained: "As God requires every man to love him with all his heart, soul, mind, and strength, and his neighbour as himself; then he is a perfect man that does so; *he answers the need for which God made him*" (emphasis added).[2]

Underscore in your thought that last phrase, and you have the essence of holiness. As a *commandment* of God, perfect love is the substance of the law; as a *promise* of God, it is the quintessence of the gospel.

The Promise

As the law is in the New Testament ("Be perfect, therefore, as your heavenly Father is perfect" [Matt. 5:48, NIV]), so the gospel is in the Old Testament: "The LORD your God will circumcise your hearts and the hearts of your descendants, so that you may love him with all your heart and with all your soul, and live" (Deut. 30:6, NIV). What God *commands* in the law He promises to *do* in the gospel. In Old Testament times, circumcision was an outward sign that the person belonged to God. But God also wanted to give His people an *inward* sign, an inward change, that would mark them as His.

Though the metaphor "circumcision of the heart" is fraught with patriarchal baggage, the message comes through that a heart filled with love to God and neighbor is His will for all of us. The Old Testament prophet Joel declared that both "sons and daughters" would be filled with the Spirit (see 2:28).

At the very heart of the gospel is the promise of a deeper working of God's grace in the heart of the Christian believer, a grace receivable by faith in this present moment, enabling us to *be* and to *act* in conformity to the great commandment, which is to love God supremely and to love every other person as we love our own souls!

When John Wesley explained to Edmund Gibson, bishop of London, his doctrine of perfection as perfect love, "without any reserve or disguise," the bishop's response was, "Mr. Wesley, if this be what you mean, publish it in all the world."[3]

This is indeed good news! God can remove the uncircumcised heart—the stubborn, rebellious heart—and give to each of us a tender, pliable heart that says, "I delight to do thy will, O my God" (Ps. 40:8, KJV).

Not Perfectionism

We must distinguish between Christian perfection and "perfectionism." This distinction we have not always made, to the confusion of many who, in the late Edward Lawlor's words, "take pains and give them to everybody else" in trying to be "perfect." No wonder so many say, "I was better when I didn't try!"

Under these conditions, it is easy to succumb to what Bonhoeffer called "cheap grace" and "throw out the baby with the bathwater"!

Holiness is not the "second effort"; it is "the second rest." A believer who has yielded utterly to God and has received the infilling of the Holy Spirit is not uptight, trying to dot every *i* and cross every *t* in order to please God. For this person, life is a perpetual Sabbath of worship, praise, and service in the Spirit of Jesus. As the author of Hebrews writes, "There remains, then, a Sabbath-rest for the people of God; for anyone who enters God's rest also rests from his own work, just as God did from his" (4:9-10, NIV).

> *Blessed quietness! Holy quietness!*
> *What assurance in my soul!*
> *On the stormy sea Jesus speaks to me,*
> *And the billows cease to roll.*
> —Manie Payne Ferguson

A "Habitual Disposition" of Love

Following Thomas Aquinas, Wesley declared that
Christian perfection is "that habitual disposition of soul,
which, in the sacred writings, is termed holiness."[4] It is a
"habitual disposition," not habitual perfect performance.
That is why the plea for forgiveness in the Lord's Prayer
(see Matt. 6:12) is not foreign to perfection; rather, it is a
sign of it.

As members of Adam's fallen race, our habitual disposition is that of inordinate, idolatrous self-love. We are born,
as Luther noted, "curved in on ourselves." We are born *psy-
chocentric*, and we grow up *egocentric*. Each of us by nature
wants to be the center of the universe, that is to say, God.

This idolatrous "heart of stone" is the essence of original sin. But God has given this promise: "I will remove
from you your heart of stone and give you a heart of flesh.
And I will put my Spirit in you and move you to follow
my . . . laws" (Ezek. 36:26-27, NIV). Then we joyfully sing,

> I'll say yes, Lord, yes
> to Your will and to Your way.
> I'll say yes, Lord, yes;
> I will trust You and obey.
> When Your Spirit speaks to me,
> With my whole heart I'll agree,
> And my answer will be
> yes, Lord, yes.*

Perfect Love, Not Sinlessness

Fundamental to Wesley's teaching is the distinction
between "the perfect law" of love (as delineated in 1 Cor.
13 and the Sermon on the Mount) and "perfect love" (understood as "pure love to God and man," or singleness of
intention). Even those perfected in love "fall short of the

glory of God" and are, therefore, with every other Christian "justified freely by his grace through the redemption that came by Christ Jesus . . . apart from observing the law" (Rom. 3:23, 24, 28, NIV).

This distinction explains Wesley's doctrine of the double nature of actual sin. His primary definition of sin is "every voluntary breach of the law of love . . . and nothing else."[5] But after spelling out the *perfect law of love* in 1 Cor. 13, Wesley writes, "You who feel all love, compare yourselves with the preceding description. Weigh yourselves in this balance, and see if you are not wanting in many particulars."[6]

Wesley believed that sin is "every voluntary breach of the law of love . . . and nothing else."

Because even those who enjoy perfect love still fall short of "the perfect law" of love, *"sinless perfection,"* Wesley says, "is a phrase I never use, lest I should seem to contradict myself."[7] Christian perfection is salvation from sin—from its *power* or *dominion* in the new birth and its *root* (false self-centeredness) in full salvation—but it is not sinlessness, since "the best of [persons] . . . com[e] short of the law of love" and therefore always "need the atonement."[8] It is therefore appropriate, as long as we live, to say with Charles Wesley,

> *Every moment, Lord, I need*
> *The merit of Thy death.*[9]

In one word, Christian perfection is a *Christ-centered* existence. In his *A Plain Account of Christian Perfection*, Wesley insists,

> The holiest of [persons] still need Christ, as their Prophet, as "the light of the world." For He does not give them light, but from moment to moment; the instant He

withdraws, all is darkness. They still need Christ as their King; for God does not give them a stock of holiness. But unless they receive a supply every moment, nothing but unholiness would remain. They still need Christ as their Priest, to make atonement for their holy things. Even perfect holiness is acceptable to God only through Jesus Christ.[10]

Such a Christian's confession is, therefore, "Thou art my light, my holiness, my heaven. Through my union with Thee, I am full of light, of holiness, and happiness. But if I were left to myself, I should be nothing but sin, darkness, hell."[11]

Lelia N. Morris expresses this truth pictorially when she writes:

> *"Called unto holiness," praise His dear name!*
> *This blessed secret to faith now made plain:*
> *Not our own righteousness, but Christ within,*
> *Living, and reigning, and saving from sin.*

In the chapters that follow, we will search the Scriptures to see if these things are true (see Acts 17:11) and, if so, to examine their implications for Christian living today.

O FLAME OF LOVE

> *O Flame of love and holiness,*
> *Thou dost indwell my heart;*
> *But grant to me the lowliness*
> *That was the Master's part.*
>
> *O Pentecostal Life of joy,*
> *O Brightness of my day,*
> *Thou givest peace without alloy,*
> *And lightest all my way.*
>
> *Thee I would praise while life shall last;*
> *Thee I would own and serve,*
> *Would day by day before Thee cast*
> *Myself without reserve.*
>   —J. Kenneth Grider

Light for Your Spiritual Journey

Cornerstones

This chapter stands on four foundational cornerstones:

1. The promise of Deut. 30:6 and the command of Matt. 5:48.
2. The difference between *perfectio* (Latin) and *teleios* (Greek).
3. Idolatrous self-love is our sickness, but it is a sickness God wants to cure.
4. Even the most holy Christians need the atonement of Jesus every moment.

Review the chapter and think about the above cornerstones. Try to write out in your own words the meaning of each one in a sentence or two. Imagine that you need to explain them to a 12-year-old child. If you take time to put just one of the cornerstones into the language level of children, select No. 2. If you actually explain it to a child and want to know whether it got through or not, ask the child to explain it back to you.

Spiritual Stepping-stones

1. How did this chapter make you feel?

___ *a.* surprised   ___ *d.* guilty

___ *b.* relieved   ___ *e.* encouraged

___ *c.* cheated   ___ *f.* (other) _____

2. If there is one life-changing idea in this chapter, it is that _____.

3. The essence of holiness, according to Greathouse and Adam Clarke, is "to answer the end for which God made" us. Are you living out God's purpose for your life? Does this question prompt you to *praise* or to *pray?*

4. Author Greathouse used the example of a pen to illustrate the Bible meaning of perfection. A pen is *perfect,* not because it is flawless, but because it writes—it does what it was designed to do. Can you give additional examples?

5. If you are writing a story with the pen that is your life, is it the story that God had in mind for you?

What is the chapter you have written so far this year?

What will the next chapter be about?

What erasing, editing, changes need to be made in the current story of your life?

When will you make them or let God make them?

Tools to Work With

1. This chapter contains quotations from five hymns or poems. Select one or two of these to use every day this week in your private devotions as prayers or objects for recitation and meditation.

2. Is there something in this chapter that you should share with a family member or friend?

3. Self-love is the disease of original sin. Examine your heart before God, and pray that love of God and neighbor will come to characterize your life.

Use the following classical prayer for perfect love. Pray it every morning and every evening. Pray it as you begin and end your study of each chapter in this book.

A Prayer for Perfect Love
*Almighty God, to whom all hearts
be open, all desires known,
and from whom no secrets are hid,
Cleanse the thoughts of our hearts
By the inspiration of Thy Holy Spirit,
That we may perfectly love Thee
And worthily magnify Thy holy name,
Through Jesus Christ our Lord, Amen.*[12]

Holy, holy, holy is the LORD *Almighty; the whole earth is full of his glory.*

—Isa. 6:3, NIV

2

The Old Testament Roots of Holiness Teaching

FOR MANY CONTEMPORARY CHRISTIANS THE OLD Testament seems ancient and remote. Therefore, we are not too much concerned about our ignorance of it. If we really want to be Christians, the Old Testament seems outdated by the New.

Yet the truth is that we cannot really understand the New Testament without a knowledge of the Old. The roots of our Christian faith lie deep in the soil of the Old. Observed Augustine, "The New is in the Old concealed; the Old is in the New revealed." This observation is true of the doctrine of Christian holiness. The New Testament doctrine of sanctification is the flower of Old Testament teaching.

What's in a Word

The place to begin is with the word *holiness*, but to understand this term, we don't turn to an English-language dictionary. Rather, with the help of scholars, we must look at the Hebrew word *qodesh*. "This is the most intimately divine word of all," says Norman H. Snaith; "it has to do with the very nature of Deity; no word more so, nor any other as much."[1]

An examination of the usage of this term reveals that it has three interrelated meanings. It carries within it the ideas of separation (or "separateness"), glory, and purity. While *qodesh* is an ancient word, it is filled with meaning for those of us who yearn to obey the divine command "Be ye holy; for I am holy" (1 Pet. 1:16, KJV).

The Separate One

The 830 instances in which *qodesh* or one of its cognates appears reveal that its primary meaning is "separation." This idea is common to every instance in which the term occurs in the Old Testament scriptures. God alone is *qodesh;* persons or things are *qodesh* only as they are related to Him.

Holiness is not merely one of the divine attributes, or even its chiefest; it is the very nature of God. When the prophet Amos says that "the Lord GOD has sworn by His holiness" (4:2, NKJV), he is saying the same thing as he declares later: "The Lord GOD has sworn by Himself" (6:8, NKJV).[2] God is *qodesh* in himself. Whatever else the sovereign Lord subsequently makes known of himself is governed by the fact that He is the holy God, the "Wholly Other."[3]

The first truth, therefore, to settle in our thinking is that of the absolute and final distinction between God and us creatures. "I am God and no mortal," the sovereign Lord announces, "the Holy One in your midst" (Hos. 11:9).

To blur the difference between God and ourselves is the root of all sin. Such a breakdown occurred in the dawn of history when the serpent promised Adam and Eve that if they would assert their independence of God, they would themselves "be like God" in deciding what is good and what is evil (Gen. 3:5). Self-sovereignty is still *the sin* of humankind. It is the distinctive sin and scandal of current New Age thought.

But if to blur the distinction between Deity and ourselves is the root of all sin, to "let God be God" is the root of all holiness.

The first word of holiness is, therefore, "I, I am the LORD, and besides me there is no savior" (Isa. 43:11). God—alone—is God; the creature—alone—is creature. This qualitative distinction between God and creature is the axiom of all holiness. As Snaith insists, "God is separate and distinct because He is God. A person or thing may be separate, or may come to be separated, because he or it has come to belong to God."[4] While holiness is separation from all sin, even more significantly it is separation to God.[5]

Do I long to be holy as God is holy? Then let me never forget that, as my Redeemer, God alone has rightful claim to my total allegiance and undivided worship.

> *O grant that nothing in my soul*
>   *May dwell, but Thy pure love alone;*
> *O may Thy love possess me whole,*
>   *My joy, my treasure, and my crown.*
> *Strange fires far from my heart remove;*
> *My every act, word, thought, be love.*[6]

The Separate One, "Glorious in Holiness"

While separation is the primary meaning of *qodesh*, in many instances it is synonymous with *kabod*, or glory, "in the sense of the burning splendour of the presence of the Lord."[7] The "Wholly Other" shines with an ineffable radiance, beauty, or glory that is His alone. "Who is like unto thee, O LORD . . . ? who is like thee, glorious in holiness . . . ?" (Exod. 15:11, KJV), we join in singing with Moses and the children of Israel.

Numerous passages link God's holiness with His glory.[8] At the burning bush, Moses was told he was standing on "holy ground" (Exod. 3:5). Aflame with God's presence and burning holiness, Mount Sinai was described as holy and inaccessible (see 19:23-24). Promising to be with His people in the Tabernacle, God said, "I will meet with the Israelites there, and it shall be sanctified by my glory" (29:43). And when Moses had finished its construction, "The cloud covered the Tent of Meeting, and the glory of the LORD filled the tabernacle" (40:34, NIV). Likewise, upon the dedication of the Temple in Jerusalem that replaced the former tent of meeting, "the glory of the LORD filled the house of the LORD" (1 Kings 8:11, NKJV). The divine Shechinah marked the presence of the holy God among His people. It still does! The Shechinah is what Phineas F. Bresee urged upon an infant denomination when he said, "Keep the glory down!"

"The radiant presence or glory of the holy God," George Allen Turner writes, "expresses the innermost nature of Deity."[9] When the "Wholly Other" wholly possesses and fills my being, "my soul is filled with glory!" (J. M. Harris). "The burning splendour of the presence of the Lord," as expressed above by Norman Snaith, suffuses my heart and life. And then I become "the temple of the Lord," my poor heart becoming the "holy of holies," where the Shechinah of God now condescends to dwell.

The Separate One, Blazing in Purity

Rounding out the meaning of *qodesh* is God's blazing purity. Separateness, glory, and purity—these comprise the nature of the Holy One. It is in the prophet Isaiah's vision of the divine holiness recorded in the sixth chapter of his book that we see the full disclosure of this truth.

The prophet begins, "In the year that King Uzziah died, I saw the Lord seated on a throne, high and exalted, and the train of his robe filled the temple" (6:1, NIV). Here is the transcendent, incomparable God, the "Wholly Other" who alone is "high and exalted" above all creation and creatures (see 40:9-31).

"Above him were seraphs," Isaiah continues, "each with six wings" (v. 2, NIV). As the seraphs sing "Holy, holy, holy," they cover their faces, so that they may not see God, and their feet, so that He might not behold them. Thus they move about the throne, proclaiming to one another the holiness of God[10]—"Holy, holy, holy is the LORD Almighty; the whole earth is full of his glory" (v. 3, NIV).

—

**The prophet was struck dumb
by both his creatureliness and
his sinfulness. And we will be too.**

—

While God is the "Wholly Other," He is not "*wholly* 'wholly other.'"[11] The transcendent Deity bathes His creation with His glory. He is immanent as well as transcendent. And when we are sensitized to Him, we see, as William Blake described it, "heaven in a wild flower." Every creature both small and great, every valley and every mountain, every human being whatever the race, color, or culture, in a peculiar way reflects God's glory. But above all, every heart filled with the Spirit and with praise and thanksgiving to God the Father is suffused with His glory.

"At the sound of their voices," Isaiah wants us to know, "the doorposts and thresholds shook and the temple was filled with smoke. 'Woe to me!' I cried. 'I am ruined! For I am a man of unclean lips, and I live among a people of unclean lips, and my eyes have seen the King, the LORD Almighty'" (6:4-5, NIV). The prophet was struck dumb by both his creatureliness and his sinfulness. And we will be too.

How desperately we need such a vision of the holy God in our day! In our culture, a chatty familiarity with "the Man upstairs" has displaced the speechless awe that dares not move in the presence of the Almighty. In the

Church of Jesus Christ a *horizontal* rejoicing that we are "part of the family of God" (as precious as this is) threatens to displace the *vertical* dimension of Spirit-anointed worship that with great feeling intones, "Holy, holy, holy! Lord God Almighty!" (Reginald Heber).

"Then one of the seraphs flew to me," Isaiah continues, "with a live coal in his hand, which he had taken with tongs from the altar. With it he touched my mouth and said, 'See, this has touched your lips; your guilt is taken away and your sin atoned for'" (6:6-7, NIV).

God's holiness is not a static thing. The holy God is the living, active, sovereign Lord, always dynamically present with us as the sanctifying Spirit if we truly worship Him in confession, surrender, and adoring trust. "If we confess our sins, he is faithful and just, and will forgive our sins and cleanse us from all unrighteousness" (1 John 1:9, RSV).

In our culture, a chatty familiarity with "the Man upstairs" has displaced the speechless awe that dares not move in the presence of the Almighty.

"Then," the prophet concludes, "I heard the voice of the Lord saying, 'Whom shall I send? And who will go for us?' And I said, 'Here am I. Send me!'" (6:8, NIV).

In Isaiah's Temple experience we have an anticipation of the Pentecostal outpouring of the Holy Spirit. What Moses and Isaiah and a select company of Old Testament saints found in God's holy presence is now the promise for every one of us under the terms of the new covenant. "And all of us, with unveiled faces, seeing the glory of the Lord as though reflected in a mirror, are being transformed into the same image from one degree of glory to another;

for this comes from the Lord, the Spirit" (2 Cor. 3:18). It is for us all today!

> *Oh, that in me the sacred fire*
> *Might now begin to glow,*
> *Burn up the dross of base desire,*
> *And make the mountains flow!*
>
> *Oh, that it now from heav'n might fall,*
> *And all my sins consume!*
> *Come, Holy Ghost, for Thee I call;*
> *Spirit of Burning, come!*
>
> *Refining Fire, go through my heart;*
> *Illuminate my soul;*
> *Scatter Thy life through ev'ry part,*
> *And sanctify the whole.*
>
> —Charles Wesley

Light for Your Spiritual Journey

Cornerstones

Establish the cornerstones of this chapter by finding the answers to these questions:

1. (Check all that apply.) According to this chapter, God is
   ___ a. a backslapping Buddy.
   ___ b. different from and far above mere mortals.
   ___ c. the unmoved Mover.
   ___ d. a being of burning splendor and glory.
   ___ e. in us, and we are becoming gods.
   ___ f. the "Man upstairs."
   ___ g. a being of blazing purity.

2. (Check all that apply). Isaiah was struck "numb and dumb" when he encountered God because
   a. what he saw was different from what he had been taught about God.
   b. he realized his own mere creatureliness.
   c. he became stricken with the sinfulness of his people as well as with his own inner sinfulness.
   d. he was afraid God would give him an assignment that he would not like.

3. According to author Greathouse, God pours out His glory upon
   a. all creation.
   b. believers.
   c. those who are filled with the Spirit.
   d. All of the above.
   e. None of the above.

4. According to Isa. 6, our sinfulness
   a. is terminal and hopeless.
   b. is subject to divine cleansing.
   c. is something that keeps us close to God.
   d. needs to be cleansed before we can serve God at our best.

Having answered these questions, you are now ready to state the four cornerstones of this chapter in your own words. They are

1. _____
   _____

2. _____
   _____

3. _____
   _____

4. _____
   _____

Spiritual Stepping-stones

1. This chapter refers to Moses' encounter with God at the burning bush. Moses stood on holy ground. Think now about your own "holy ground" experiences. How would you describe them? Would *glory, light, blazing purity, high and lofty, smoke, fire*—the terms used in Isa. 6 and this chapter—be something like your experience?

2. Isaiah's response to the vision of God can be described with such terms as *humility, confession, repentance, consecration, longing for purity,* and *an eagerness to serve.* In your own "holy ground" experiences, which of those terms most nearly describes your responses?

3. We cannot summon the God of the universe to appear so we can see His glory. He, the seeking God, confronts us when He will. But if we are never available to turn our hearts heavenward, maybe we are missing some encounters. Why do you think your "holy ground" experiences are so few? Too many soap operas, too much sports on television, moral guilt, three jobs? What can you do this week to make yourself more available to the Spirit of God?

4. In ancient times the holy glory of God was believed to be primarily in the holy of holies or behind the veil in the Tabernacle or Temple. On the Day of Atonement when the high priest—and only he—was to enter the sacred precinct to make an offering for the sins of the people, a rope was tied around his ankle. If the blazing holiness of God killed him, they could then pull him out without going in and losing their own lives.

We don't have to do this anymore. Review the chapter and discover why.

Tools to Work With

1. Do not make the mistake of thinking that God pours out (suffuses) His glory only in private encounters such as the Isa. 6 and Moses accounts. Included in this chapter are two examples of times when God poured out His glory on whole congregations. Read Exod. 40:34 and 1 Kings 8:11 in your devotions. Then read Acts 2.

2. How do you yourself reflect God's glory? No false modesty, please. This chapter affirms that all of us have received His glory. How does He glory in you? What about you can be called His glory?

People may justly call you weak, disloyal, thief, sinner, failure, backslider. But you are more than that—you also bear the image and glory of God. John Wesley declared that there are some remains of the image of God in the very worst of people.

Instead of always beating up on yourself and calling yourself names, why not prayerfully thank God for the part of you that bears His image?

3. In your devotions this week use "A Prayer for Perfect Love," quoted at the end of chapter 1, and the Charles Wesley hymn quoted at the close of this chapter.

*Live always in my presence
and be perfect.*
—Gen. 17:1, NEB

3

On to Perfection
The Old Testament Roots of the Doctrine of Christian Perfection

NOBODY'S PERFECT."

Say that in a loud voice, and just about everybody in any audience will nod approval. All their lives they have been dismissing their moral failures with this worldly dictum, "Nobody's perfect."

But that notion does not come from the Bible. The Holy Scriptures are not bashful in calling God's people to perfection. But what on earth do the authors of Genesis, Matthew, and Ephesians (to name a few) mean when they set perfection as the standard?

As with the teaching of holiness, the doctrine of Christian perfection is best approached by examining its Old Testament roots. As a recent church council puts it, "Most essential concepts of the Christian creed grew at first in Judaic soil. Uprooted from that soil, these basic concepts cannot be perfectly understood."[1] This is eminently true of the concept of perfection.

More than a dozen words are translated *perfect* in the King James Version of the Old Testament. In their various shades of meaning, they are applied to persons who, in light of the ethical thinking of their day, endeavored to obey God's call to Abraham: "Walk before me, and be thou perfect" (Gen. 17:1, KJV).

An open-minded reading of the Old Testament leads to the conclusion that the idea of spiritual perfection—understood as blamelessness before God and uprightness of heart and life—lies at the heart of Hebrew piety. This concept is the root of the New Testament teaching of perfection. And it is the understanding of perfection that found expression in the writings of the great saints and teachers of both Eastern Orthodoxy and Roman Catholicism and came to Protestant formulation in the thought and teaching of John Wesley.

Let's examine the Old Testament roots of this distinctive tenet of our Wesleyan faith.

Holiness and Perfection

While the terms *holiness* and *perfection* are used to describe the same experience of grace, an examination of these two terms in the older testament reveals that they reflect two different aspects of this grace. George Allen Turner explains, "While the terms associated with 'holiness' stress the contrast between Jehovah and man, which can be bridged by an act of cleansing, those associated with 'perfection' point to man's kinship with God and the possibility of fellowship."[2]

Modern versions translate the several Hebrew words rendered *perfect* in the King James Version by such terms as *blameless, whole, sincere, upright,* and *upright in heart* to avoid the misleading connotations of our English word *perfect* that suggest a state of grace we will not know until we get to heaven. These and kindred terms help us understand what John Wesley believed to be the scriptural idea of perfection.

Relative Perfection

Only in five instances, in which the reference is to God, is *perfect* used in the strictest sense (Deut. 32:4; 2 Sam. 22:31; Job 37:16; Pss. 18:30; 19:7). Only God is absolutely perfect; we are relatively "perfect" as we "walk with God" in sincerity and fidelity. "Enoch walked with God; and he was not, for God took him" (Gen. 5:24, RSV). And "before his translation he had this testimony, that he pleased God" (Heb. 11:5, KJV). Of Noah we read he "found favor in the sight of the LORD. . . . Noah was a righteous man, blameless ['perfect,' KJV] in his generation; Noah walked with God" (Gen. 6:8-9).

Two points must be noted. First, it is only "before God" that Noah and other Hebrews were "perfect." Second, this perfection was relative to the ethical standards of their generation. In contrast to his neighbors, Noah was "righteous." But judged by God's perfect law, he fell far short (just as we do!). Perfection among us mortals is always relative to our finite understanding of God's law.

Explaining John Wesley's doctrine, Colin Williams wisely observes: "In terms of sin in the absolute sense, as measured by the 'perfect law,' there is no such thing as perfection in believers. It is in terms of the sin of conscious separation from Christ that there can be perfection—*a perfection of unbroken conscious dependence upon Christ*" (emphasis added).[3]

"Godly Sincerity"

"Godly sincerity" is, therefore, an appropriate synonym for "perfection" in Scripture (see Josh. 24:14; 2 Cor. 1:12). Of course, one can be sincerely wrong and go to hell! But you cannot be insincere and enjoy the fellowship of the Holy One and the cleansing of Jesus' blood. These promised blessings demand that we "walk in the light, as he is in the light" (1 John 1:7, KJV; see John 1:5-9).

For Wesley, sincerity was a premium. The 1746 Methodist Conference Minutes are explicit:

Q. Whom do you term sincere?

A. One who walks in the light as God is in the light. . . .

Q. Is not [sincerity] all in all?

A. God gives everything with it, nothing without it. . . .

Q. But do we not [then] set sincerity on the level of faith? . . .

A. No, . . . we do not put it in the place of faith. It is by faith the merits of Christ are applied to the soul, but if I am not sincere they are not applied.[4]

"Godly sincerity" is an appropriate synonym for "perfection."

Note Paul's testimony to the Corinthians: "For our boast is this, the testimony of our conscience that we have behaved in the world, and still more toward you, with holiness and *godly sincerity*, not by earthly wisdom but by the grace of God" (2 Cor. 1:12, RSV, emphasis added).

A Single Intention

In the Sermon on the Mount, Jesus cautioned that we beware of practicing our piety before others "to be seen by them" (Matt. 6:1). Rather, we must give, pray, and fast in the sight of God alone (see vv. 1-18). "If therefore thine eye be single, thy whole body shall be full of light," He says. "But if thine eye be evil, thy whole body shall be full of darkness" (vv. 22-23, KJV).

The term "single eye," says Richard Foster, has a rich connotation: "It refers both to a single aim in life and to a generous unselfish spirit. The two ideas have such a close connection in the Hebrew mind that they can be expressed by a single phrase."[5]

John Wesley comments, "What the eye is to the body, the intention is to the soul. . . . 'If thine eye be single,' singly fixed upon God, 'thy whole body' . . . shall be filled with holiness and happiness."[6] The "perfect" Christian is one who does "everything for the glory of God" (1 Cor. 10:31). Singleness of intention is a classic definition of perfection. Søren Kierkegaard put it unforgettably: "Purity of heart is to will one thing—the Good."[7]

Blamelessness and Wholeness

The Lord appeared to Abraham and said, "I am God Almighty; walk before me, and be blameless" (Gen. 17:1; see NASB, NIV, NKJV, RSV). My Old Testament professor, J. Philip Hyatt, insisted God was saying in this verse, "Walk before me in integrity." The Hebrew *tamîm* suggests the idea of being "blameless" as well as "complete, whole, having integrity."[8] Two modern versions retain "perfect," which carries within it both meanings. The *New English Bible* says, "Live always in my presence and be perfect." Similarly, the *New Jerusalem Bible* reads, "Live in my presence, be perfect." It is in the gracious, empowering presence of El Shaddai that Abraham would be enabled to be "perfect." Perfection is complete openness to God.

Blamelessness is an oft-recurring concept in the New Testament.[9] Perfection is not faultlessness before others, it is blamelessness before God. God has chosen us in Christ "to be holy and blameless before him in love" (Eph. 1:4). The Greek word *(amōmos)* is a sacrificial term. An animal offered in sacrifice was to be "whole," "without blemish," "with no part left out."[10] To be *amōmos* as Christians means that our whole person must be offered to God. As Barclay says, "It *[amōmos]* thinks of taking every part of our life, work, pleasure, sport, home life, personal relationships and making them all such that they can be offered to God. This word does not mean that the Christian must be respectable; it means that he must be perfect. . . . It means that the Christian standard is nothing less than perfection."[11] And Paul assures us that for the Church Christ gave himself "so that she may be holy and without blemish" (Eph. 5:27).

Another important synonym for perfection, found about 160 times, is "uprightness."[12] It is applied to both God and to men who are "upright in heart" (6 times: Pss. 7:10; 11:2; 32:11; 36:10; 64:10; 94:15). The verb form means "to please, to be right in the sight of" God.[13]

The Paradox of Perfection

While the Book of Job addresses the problem of unjust suffering, it is also a treatise on perfection. It opens with the categorical claim that Job was a man "blameless ['perfect,' KJV] and upright, one who feared God and turned away from evil" (1:1).

Although Satan admits Job's uprightness, he is cynical about Job's motive: "Does Job fear God for nothing? Have you not put a fence around him? . . . But stretch out your hand now, and touch all that he has, and he will curse you to your face" (vv. 9-11). The unleashed forces of evil then began to batter Job. While his "friends" taunted him with accusations of wrongdoing (Otherwise why would God be punishing him? they reasoned), Job steadfastly maintained his integrity. Although he felt abandoned from God's presence in the depths of his trials and sufferings (see 23:1-10), yet he could say, "I have not departed from the commandment of his lips; I have treasured in my bosom the words of his mouth" (v. 12). Satan was wrong; Job's was a disinterested love that could say, "Though he kill me, yet I will trust in him" (13:15, margin). He was indeed perfect!

Nevertheless, when he beheld God in His majestic holiness, Job's lips were silenced. Then he could only say: "Now my eye sees you; therefore I despise myself, and repent in dust and ashes" (42:5-6). The final proof of Job's perfection was the admission of his folly and shortcomings. To see and feel the full weight of this paradox is to acknowledge with Charles Wesley,

> *Every moment, Lord, I need*
> *The merit of Thy death.*

Light for Your Spiritual Journey

Cornerstones

1. Godly Sincerity

In a commencement speech at Meredith College in Raleigh, North Carolina, Erma Bombeck said, "Never confuse fame and success. Madonna is one; Mother Teresa is the other."

Paul wrote, "The testimony of our conscience [is] that we have behaved . . . with holiness and godly sincerity, not by earthly wisdom but by the grace of God" (2 Cor. 1:12, RSV). Samuel Goldwyn said, "The secret of success is sincerity. Once you fake that, you've got it made."[14]

One cornerstone of Christian perfection is godly sincerity. The gaps between

Madonna and Mother Teresa

Paul and Samuel Goldwyn

reveal what godly sincerity and its opposite look like in real life.

2. Integrity, blamelessness, and wholeness form another cornerstone of biblical perfection.

Jean-Jacques Rousseau, the Swiss-French moralist, in his classic book *Émile* wrote about the education of children. His philosophy of parenting was that a child must be allowed to develop in a wholesome atmosphere protected from corrupting influences.

While Mr. Rousseau was being praised for his wonderful book, almost no one realized that he preached one thing and lived another. Seventeen years before *Émile* was published in 1762, Rousseau took a hotel maid, Theresa le Vasseur, as his lifelong mistress. She bore him five children. And each one he put into a primitive foundling home right after his or her birth. In 1768 he finally married Theresa—but he had already given away all their children.

Integrity is one cornerstone of Christian perfection. Rousseau modeled its opposite. Think about a Christian that you have known who modeled (or models) integrity.

3. **Singleness of heart**—willing one thing—**and purity of intention** form another cornerstone of biblical perfection. Read again what this chapter has to say about this subject. In your observations, reading, and memory try to think of positive and negative real-life examples that model the gap between singleness of heart and its opposite.

Spiritual Stepping-stones

The state of California conducted case studies of 200 violent criminals. Without exception, they all insisted that they were *good*. Not one accepted the label *evil*.

We might be able to fool a sociologist doing case studies, but we seldom fool ourselves, and we never fool God.

Read Ps. 139:23-24 and ask God to lead you into a deeper experience of godly sincerity, integrity, and purity of intention.

Tools to Work With

1. Keep using "A Prayer for Perfect Love" cited in chapter 1. Add this usage for the coming week: repeat it as a table grace for one meal each day, whether you eat alone or with others.

2. Start and close each day this week by reading or singing these words from a hymn by Charles Wesley:

What is our calling's glorious hope
*   But inward holiness?*
For this to Jesus I look up,
*   I calmly wait for this.*
I wait till He shall touch me clean,
*   Shall life and power impart,*
Give me the faith that casts out sin
*   And purifies the heart.*

This is the dear redeeming grace,
*   For every sinner free;*
Surely it shall in me take place,
*   The chief of sinners, me.*
. . . .
Be it according to Thy word!
*   Redeem me from all sin;*
My heart would now receive Thee, Lord;
*   Come in, my Lord, come in!*

*"You shall love the Lord your God with
all your heart, and with all your soul,
and with all your mind."
This is the greatest and first commandment.*
—Matt. 22:37-38

4

The Love Command

IF YOU REALLY WANT TO BE CHRISTIAN—NOT
merely in name but in truth—you must understand and
come to terms with the love command of Scripture: "'You
shall love the Lord your God with all your heart, and with
all your soul, and with all your mind.' This is the greatest
and first commandment. And a second is like it: 'You shall
love your neighbor as yourself.' On these two commandments hang all the law and the prophets" (Matt. 22:37-40).

This command is not only the very heart of biblical re-
ligion but also the essence of the Judeo-Christian ethic.
Furthermore, as a "covered promise," it is everything John
Wesley meant by Christian perfection.

Moses: The Love Command, Part One

"Hear, O Israel: The LORD is our God, the LORD alone.
You shall love the LORD your God with all your heart, and
with all your soul, and with all your might" (Deut. 6:4-5).

"Hear, O Israel." The love command is addressed, not to humanity in general, but to God's redeemed people, as the introduction to the Ten Commandments makes clear: "I am the LORD your God, who brought you out of the land of Egypt, out of the house of bondage. You shall have no other gods before me" (Exod. 20:2-3, RSV). Having redeemed Israel by His grace, God makes an exclusive claim upon their worship.

The Mosaic covenant must therefore be seen as a covenant of *grace* and the Decalogue as Israel's appropriate response to that grace.

This truth is underscored in Moses' rehearsal of the Law: "It was because the LORD loved you . . . that the LORD has . . . redeemed you from the house of slavery" (Deut. 7:8). Therefore, "You shall love the Lord your God with all your heart" (Matt. 22:37).

From the beginning, covenant love has been the essence of holiness: human love responding in radical obedience to God's redeeming love. To miss this truth inevitably leads to loveless legalism.

━━

The lurking self-idolatry of the unsanctified heart creates a host of idols before which we foolishly bow down and waste ourselves.

━━

The radical obedience commanded by the Lord is the willing recognition of His absolute claim upon our hearts and lives. "You shall not make for yourself an idol . . . for I the LORD your God am a jealous God" (Exod. 20:4-5). Since "the LORD alone" is God, we must worship Him alone.

Wallace Hamilton, however, speaks for many Christians when he says, "We are not monotheists yet, except in theory. . . . We believe in one God and spread our loyalties among the many gods. . . . The great question is sovereignty. . . . To whom does our first allegiance belong? Glibly we say, 'To God.' But practically we say, 'To many gods.'"[1]

Idolatry, Luther observes, is the sin of any heart in which God does not rule alone. The lurking self-idolatry of the unsanctified heart creates a host of idols—unholy ambition, greed, lust, and so on—before which we foolishly bow down and waste ourselves. Lord, is it I? "Search me, O God, and know my heart; test me and know my thoughts" (Ps. 139:23).

> *The dearest idol I have known,*
> *Whate'er that idol be,*
> *Help me to tear it from Thy throne*
> *And worship only Thee.*
>
> —William Cowper

The Love Command, Part Two

In His summation of the Law, Jesus cited as a second great commandment a verse from the Holiness Code in Leviticus: "You shall love your neighbor as yourself" (19:18).

This second half of the love command is not second in importance. The truth is, you cannot love God if you do not love your neighbor. "The commandment we have from him is this: those who love God must love their brothers and sisters also" (1 John 4:21). The love command is one command in two dimensions.

Inordinate self-love, however, blinds us to the divine obligation of neighbor love. My first college president, A. K. Bracken, one day said in chapel, "Some people seem never to have discovered that the world is chiefly populated by *others!*"

Until God crushes the hard shell that encases me in my egocentricity and releases me to love others as I love myself, I am not living up to the standard of New Testament religion. Those "others" must also include those who would be my enemies.

At the heart of the Sermon on the Mount is this strong word: "Love your enemies and pray for those who persecute you, so that you may be children of your Father in heaven; for he makes his sun rise on the evil and on the good, and sends rain on the righteous and on the unrighteous. . . . Be perfect, therefore [in love for enemy as well as friend], as your heavenly Father is perfect" (Matt. 5:44-45, 48).

The perfect love Jesus commands is not *feeling*, which we cannot command. It is the spirit of forgiveness and goodwill that refuses to nurse our hurts and grievances or harbor resentments. It is the spirit of Jesus, who prayed for His crucifiers, "Father, forgive them; for they know not what they do" (Luke 23:34, KJV).

Such Christlike love is what John Wesley meant by holiness of heart. In his sermon "The Scripture Way of Salvation," Wesley defines entire sanctification as "love excluding sin, love filling the heart, taking up the whole capacity of the soul. . . . How clearly does this express the being perfected in love!—how strongly imply being saved from all sin!" Wesley elaborates. "For as long as love takes up the whole heart, what room is there for sin therein?"[2]

This, then, is the love command: that we give God our undivided and wholehearted devotion and that we express in all our human relationships the caring, forgiving, and merciful love of our Heavenly Father.

Jesus: The Love Command Fulfilled

Jesus is the only one who has perfectly obeyed the love command and thereby fulfilled God's Law. He was the perfect Embodiment of the Law, not only negatively in His sinlessness but just as significantly, fleshing out positively what it means to love God absolutely and one's neighbor as oneself. Jesus was God's Law—the law of love—incarnate. Theologians speak of this as Jesus' *active* righteousness.

But as the holy Lamb of God, He fulfilled the Law in a second way, by offering himself up as the atoning Sacrifice for the sins of the world. In the Epistle to the Hebrews we read, "By one sacrifice he has made perfect forever those who are being made holy" (10:14, NIV). Theologians speak of His sacrificial death as Jesus' *passive* righteousness.

By His sinless life and atoning sacrifice, Jesus instituted the new covenant, on the terms of which we receive the Holy Spirit, "so that the just requirement of the law might be fulfilled in us, who walk not according to the flesh but according to the Spirit" (Rom. 8:4).

In understanding the love command, it is essential that we make a distinction in our thinking between Law and gospel. Martin Luther insisted that anyone who knows the difference between the two is a theologian.

What *is* the distinction? Is it the distinction between the Old and the New Testament? No, for the Law is in the New Testament. Jesus said, "Think not that I have come to abolish the law and the prophets; I have come not to abolish them but to fulfil them" (Matt. 5:17, RSV). And as we will see, the gospel is in the Old Testament.

The Law is what God *requires;* the gospel is what He *gives.*

What, then, is the distinction between the Law and the gospel? The Law, says Luther, is what God *requires;* the gospel is what He *promises and gives.*[3]

By this definition, the heart of the gospel is Jer. 31:31-34 (which the author of Hebrews cites immediately after

his statement in 10:14 cited above). This great passage follows in part:

> But this is the covenant which I will make with the
> house of Israel after those days, says the LORD: I will put
> my law within them, and I will write it upon their hearts;
> and I will be their God, and they shall be my people.
> And no longer shall each man teach his neighbor and
> each his brother, saying, "Know the LORD," for they shall
> all know me, from the least of them to the greatest, says
> the LORD; for I will forgive their iniquity, and I will re-
> member their sin no more *(Jer. 31:33-34, RSV)*.

On the night before His passion Jesus took the cup
and said, "This is my blood of the covenant, which is
poured out for many for the forgiveness of sins" (Matt.
26:28).

The promise of the new covenant is threefold:

1. The first and most precious provision of the new
covenant is the forgiveness of our sins through the blood
of Jesus, "purify[ing] our conscience from dead works to
worship the living God!" (Heb. 9:14).

2. The very moment we are pardoned from our sins,
we "know the Lord" by the direct witness of the Spirit
(Gal. 4:6; Rom. 8:15-16).

3. Furthermore, at that same instant God begins to
write His law in our minds and hearts. "Faith alone makes
us righteous," says Luther, "and fulfills the law; for out of
Christ's merit it brings the Spirit, who makes the heart
glad and free as the law requires that it shall be."[4] This is
the beginning of *sanctification* (1 Cor. 6:11).

But while Jeremiah was announcing the new covenant
in Jerusalem, Ezekiel was proclaiming it in terms even
more radical: "I will sprinkle clean water upon you, and
you shall be clean from all your uncleannesses, and from
all your idols I will cleanse you. A new heart I will give
you, and a new spirit I will put within you; and I will take
out of your flesh the heart of stone and give you a heart of

flesh. And I will put my spirit within you, and cause you to walk in my statutes and be careful to observe my ordinances" (36:25-27, RSV).

Here indeed is the promise of a divine heart transplant! The Great Physician promises to remove our "heart of stone"—the hard core of idolatrous self-love that survives the new birth—and give to us a tender and obedient "heart of flesh" indwelt by the sanctifying Spirit!

Here indeed is the promise of a divine heart transplant!

What Ezekiel's promise means experientially is that the *disposition* of inordinate self-love that is our inheritance as members of Adam's fallen race will be displaced by "that habitual *disposition* of soul which, in the sacred writings, is termed holiness."[5]

That disposition is the mind of Christ promised in Rom. 8:1-11, which enables us to sing,

> *I'll say yes, Lord, yes*
> *to Your will and to Your way.**

Such perfection is not *perfectionism*, which strains to dot every *i* and cross every *t*. It is the disposition of heart that says, "I delight to do Thy will, O my God" (Ps. 40:8, NASB). It does not exempt us from praying, "Forgive us our trespasses, as we forgive those who trespass against us" (see Matt. 6:12, 14-15), for as long as we live we fall short of the perfect law of love and must therefore pray with Charles Wesley, "Every moment, Lord, I need / The merit of Thy death." It is not angelic perfection or absolute perfection; it is *evangelical* perfection, enabling us to fulfill "the

*"Yes, Lord, Yes" by Lynn Keesecker. © Copyright 1983 by Manna Music, Inc., 35255 Brooten Road, Pacific City, OR 97135. All rights reserved. Used by permission.

just requirement of the law," or love (Rom. 8:4; 13:8-10; Gal. 5:14).

So let us pray: *"Almighty God, unto whom all hearts are open, all desires known, and from whom no secrets are hid: cleanse the thoughts of our hearts by the inspiration of Thy Holy Spirit, that we may perfectly love Thee and worthily magnify Thy holy name, through Christ, our Lord. Amen."*[6]

Light for Your Spiritual Journey

Cornerstones

1. **Self-idolatry.** In Larkspur, California, three men tried to steal a car. The owner caught them in the act. He screamed. They ran. The owner chased them, hailing a police car as he went. The cops joined the chase. The three would-be car thieves made a desperate dash for freedom. Helping each other, they scrambled up a high chain-link fence with barbed wire at the top. Scratched and bleeding, they leaped down safely on the other side a few yards ahead of the police. The policemen smiled through the fence at the confused crooks. "Congratulations, men," one of the policemen said. "You just broke into San Quentin."

This story is a parable of life for those blinded by self-idolatry. Refusing grace, they insist on pursuing money, lust, power. They wind up scratched and bleeding in the very place they don't want to be. They break into the prison made of sinful, selfish desires.

Have you broken into any prisons lately? What does this chapter have to say about getting out of the jail of self-idolatry?

2. **The Love Command, Part One**

To love God above anything and anyone else is the clear Bible message.

Read the scriptures cited in this chapter as part of your Bible study this week:
> Matt. 22:37-40
> Deut. 6:4-5
> Deut. 7:8
> Exod. 20:1-5
> Jer. 31:33-34

3. The Love Command, Part Two

We must love our neighbor as ourselves. Read the author's comments about loving others in this chapter. Look again at
> Matt. 5:44-48
> Matt. 22:39-40
> Lev. 19:18
> 1 John 4:21

4. Jesus, Model and Redeemer

Establish this cornerstone by reflecting on the following phrases from this chapter:

- "Jesus is the only one who has perfectly obeyed the love command."
- "The world is chiefly populated by *others!*"
- "Love your enemies and pray for those who persecute you."
- "Perfect love . . . is not *feeling* . . . It is the spirit of forgiveness . . . that refuses to nurse our hurts . . . or harbor resentments."
- "The *disposition* of inordinate self-love . . . will be displaced by 'that habitual *disposition* of soul . . . termed holiness.'"
- "*Evangelical* perfection."

Spiritual Stepping-stones

1. After a person is converted, the Holy Spirit begins to work in his or her heart with the purpose of removing or cleansing remaining inward sin and filling the heart with divine love. God is faithful in this work,

readying the heart for sanctifying grace. In some cases, finding sanctifying grace takes years, in others weeks or days. How quickly it happens is not the point. Going on to perfection is the point.

God knows when you are ready. When His work in your heart brings you to the place at which you love God with all your heart, soul, mind, and strength, God will, according to John Wesley, speak the second time, "Be thou clean." (See the sermons "The Repentance of Believers" and "The Firstfruits of the Spirit.")

2. Loving others as we love ourselves is a very important spiritual stepping-stone. Think about these comments from John Wesley on this subject:

> "Thou shalt love thy neighbour as thyself." *Thou shalt love;*—Thou shalt embrace with the most tender good-will, the most earnest and cordial affection, the most inflamed desires of preventing or removing all evil, and of procuring for him every possible good. *Thy neighbour;*—that is, not only thy friend, thy kinsman . . . not only the virtuous, the friendly, him that loves thee, that . . . returns thy kindness; but every . . . human creature, every soul which God hath made; not excepting . . . him whom thou knowest to be evil and unthankful, him that . . . persecutes thee: Him thou shalt love *as thyself;* with the same invariable thirst after his happiness . . . the same unwearied care to screen him from whatever might grieve or hurt either his soul or body.[7]

This love for others is to be very active. We are to

> give to the poor; deal your bread to the hungry. Cover the naked . . . entertain the stranger; carry or send relief to them that are in prison. Heal the sick; not by miracle, but through the blessing of God upon your seasonable support. Let the blessing of him

that was ready to perish, through pining want, come upon thee. Defend the oppressed, plead the cause of the fatherless, and make the widow's heart sing for joy.[8]

Most of us, reading Wesley's standards, are moved to pray, not testify. How about you? Are you ready for a life of self-forgetfulness?

Tools to Work With

1. Inventory Quiz

a. How likely is it that the people on the job would say that I love God more than anyone or anything else?

___ (1) Very likely   ___ (3) Somewhat likely

___ (2) Likely   ___ (4) Not a chance

b. If you were being prosecuted by a hostile government because of your love for God, would there be enough evidence to convict?

c. If your immediate family members were asked what or whom you love most in the world, what would they say?

d. If anything in my life competes with God for my devotion, it is _____.

If you gave positive answers to *a-d*, take time out to praise God for His marvelous works of grace in your heart.

2. Make this hymn your prayer.

O glorious hope of perfect love!
It lifts me up to things above;
   It bears on eagles' wings;
It gives my ravished soul a taste
And makes me for some moments feast
   With Jesus' priests and kings.

Rejoicing now in earnest hope,
I stand and from the mountain-top
  See all the land below:
Rivers of milk and honey rise,
And all the fruits of Paradise
  In endless plenty grow.

O that I might at once go up!
No more on this side of Jordan stop,
  But now the land possess:
This moment end my legal years;
Sorrows, and sins, and doubts, and fears,
  A howling wilderness.

Now, O my Joshua, bring me in!
Cast out Thy foes; the inbred sin.
  The carnal mind remove;
The purchase of Thy death divide!
And oh! with all the sanctified
  Give me a lot of love.[9]

For this purpose the Son of God
was manifested, that he might destroy
the works of the devil.
—1 John 3:8, KJV

5

Christus Victor—
Our Great Savior

FOR WHAT PURPOSE DID CHRIST COME DOWN from heaven?" asks Irenaeus, the most influential of the Early Church fathers. Answer: "That he might destroy sin, overcome death, and give life to man."[1]

Going to the very heart of Early Church faith, he says again, "Our Lord bound the strong man and set free the weak, and gave salvation to his handiwork by abolishing sin."[2]

This view Gustaf Aulén calls the *Christus Victor* idea of Christ's atonement.[3] Christ died and rose, not to cover up sin, but to destroy it. His work was first and foremost a divine victory over the powers of evil that have held humanity in bondage. In His flesh-and-blood body, the Son of God, by His death and resurrection, has dethroned Satan and abolished sin and death!

The decisive victory Christ won *for* us as Jesus of Nazareth, crucified by men but raised by the Father, He gives *to* us as the exalted Lord who sends down the Holy

Spirit to continue His redemptive work *in* and *through* us until He returns in glory.

Christ's Victory *for* Us

In bold, imaginative terms, the New Testament paints Christ's victory over sin, death, and the domination of the devil. "And having disarmed the powers and authorities," we read, "he made a public spectacle of them, triumphing over them by the cross" (Col. 2:15, NIV).

Speaking of His approaching death, Jesus announced, "Now is the judgment of this world, now shall the ruler of this world be cast out" (John 12:31, RSV). "And when he comes," Jesus said of the promised Advocate, "he will convince the world . . . concerning judgment, because the ruler of this world is judged" (16:8, 11, RSV). Thank God, our ancient enemy has met his doom! Now we can enjoy present victory, "because greater is He who is in you than he who is in the world" (1 John 4:4, NASB).

Sin itself has also been potentially destroyed. "Sending his own Son in the likeness of sinful flesh and for sin, [God] condemned sin in the flesh" (Rom. 8:3, RSV). To condemn means more than to register disapproval—the Law could do that. Paul can mean only what C. H. Dodd says of this declaration: "By His life of perfect obedience, and His victorious death and resurrection, the reign of sin over human nature has been broken."[4] Thereby God, to quote John Wesley, "gave sentence that sin should be destroyed and the believer wholly delivered from it."[5]

Christ became sin for us. He sets us free. He justifies us freely. This mystery of grace is ably depicted in James Stewart's story of the Faust painting.

Faust, in the old story, gambled with his soul—and lost. In the painting Stewart describes, Faust and the devil are seated at a chessboard with Faust's soul at stake. The game in the picture is almost over. Faust has only a few pieces left—one or two pawns, a knight, and a king. On his face Faust wears a look of stark despair, while Satan leers in anticipation of his coming triumph.

The title of the painting, which hangs in a Scottish gallery, is *Checkmate*. Many a chess player has looked at that board and agreed that Faust's position is hopeless—it is checkmate.

But one day a great master of the game stood gazing at the painting. He was fascinated by the terrible despair on Faust's face. Then he stared at the pieces on the board. He gazed at them, absorbed. Other visitors in the gallery came and went, but still the chess master studied the board, lost in contemplation. Suddenly he let out a ringing shout that echoed through the gallery halls: "It's a lie! The king has another move! . . . *The king has another move!*"

I stand in the divine hall of justice, guilty, condemned, hopeless. The sentence seems inevitable. I confess my miserable sins to the court. Suddenly a voice rings out, "The King—the King of Kings has another move!" Jesus slips in and stands by my side, and in a voice as calm as a silent sea and as deep as all eternity, He says, "I became sin for him."[6]

Surely the Son of God came to destroy the works of the devil.

Further, Christ has not only potentially destroyed sin but also *potentially* sanctified every member of His Body. Irenaeus put it memorably when he wrote,

> He was made an infant for infants, sanctifying infancy; a child among children, sanctifying childhood, and setting an example of filial affection, of righteousness and obedience; a young man among young men, becoming an example to them, and sanctifying them to the Lord. So also he was a grown man among older men, . . . sanctifying the older men, and becoming an example to them also. And thus he came even to death, that he might be "the first-born from the dead," having the preeminence among all, the Author of Life, who goes before all and shows the way.[7]

And finally, by His death and resurrection, He has "brought life and immortality to light through the gospel" (2 Tim. 1:10, RSV). Through His death He has destroyed "him who holds the power of death—that is, the devil—and free[d] those who all their lives were held in slavery by their fear of death" (Heb. 2:14-15, NIV).

Such deliverance, in brief, is the glorious victory Christ has won *for* us—over Satan, sin, and death. Now let us consider

Christ's Victory *in* Us

Christ's victory becomes our victory when by penitent faith—signed and sealed by baptism—we are incorporated into Him. Every *fact* in His atoning work then becomes a *factor* in our unfolding Christian experience as we appropriate Christ himself as our life and holiness. Paul put it succinctly when he wrote, "I have been crucified with Christ; it is no longer I who live, but Christ who lives in me; and the life I now live in the flesh I live by faith in the Son of God, who loved me and gave himself for me" (Gal. 2:20, RSV).

Christ's death has become *our* death to sinning, and His life *our* new life of holiness and righteousness.

First of all, in *conversion* we die with Christ and with Him are raised to newness of life. Appropriating His death on the Cross, we are *justified*—freed from the guilt and power of sin; at the same instant we are *regenerated*—quickened with Him in the Spirit to a new life of love and holy obedience. Christ's death has become *our* death to sinning, and His life *our* new life of holiness and righteousness. This truth is in essence what Paul says in Rom. 6:1-11.

Second, in *entire sanctification* we permit Christ, who lives in us, to become sovereign Lord of our existence. As those who have been "brought from death to life" (Rom. 6:13, RSV) in regeneration, we must now "yield [ourselves] to God . . . and [our] members to God as instruments of righteousness . . . for sanctification" (vv. 13, 19, RSV). Such is Paul's urging and promise in verses 12-23 (esp. 13, 19, RSV).

Answering to this absolute abandonment of ourselves to God's sovereign claims upon us, the Spirit then fully indwells us, *making Christ our sanctifying Lord.* That claim is the substance of what Paul says in Rom. 8:1-11. Christ, who began to live in us at conversion, now *reigns* in us! In this sense entire sanctification is the actualization of our conversion. To be truly sanctified is not to be a "super" Christian; it is to be a *true* Christian.

Christ, who began to live in us at conversion, now *reigns* in us!

But let us be warned. Although we are no longer "in the flesh, [but] in the Spirit, if in fact the Spirit of God dwells in [us]" (Rom 8:9, RSV), we are still living in a *body* with urges and desires that, though not sinful in themselves, must "by the Spirit" be "put to death" (v. 13, RSV). Like the apostle himself, we must "beat [our] body and make it [our] slave" (1 Cor. 9:27, NIV). Otherwise, spiritual death may once again overtake us. Even though we may be genuinely sanctified, we are not yet glorified! This truth is Paul's reminder in Rom. 8:12-13.

It is our confident expectation, however, that our bodies will be redeemed when Christ returns in glory. Along with the entire created order, we "groan inwardly while we wait for adoption, the redemption of our bodies" (Rom.

8:23). And while we wait, we enjoy "the first fruits of the Spirit" (ibid.), a foretaste of the glory that will be ours when we see Jesus! Such is Paul's theology in verses 14-31.

This hope, however, is not just theology—it is doxology! In the Spirit we cry, "Jesus is Lord" (1 Cor. 12:3, RSV). With the angelic choir we sing, "Hallelujah! For the Lord our God the Almighty reigns" (Rev. 19:6, RSV). And with the redeemed of all ages we join in a hymn to Christ the Victor: "To him who sits upon the throne and to the Lamb be blessing and honor and glory and might for ever and ever!" (5:13, RSV).

Light for Your Spiritual Journey

Cornerstones

1. To get a broad-scoped view of the cornerstones of this chapter, study Rom. 6, 7, and 8. Read them in several translations and in the paraphrase *The Message.*

2. This chapter rests on two cornerstones: Christ's victory *for* us and Christ's victory *in* us. Try to express the core meaning of these cornerstones in one sentence each.

3. Suppose you were to give a speech, sermon, or lesson using this outline:

   a. Christ's Victory *for* Us.

   b. Christ's Victory *in* Us.

   c. What Difference Does This Make?

How would you develop the last point? Would you include conversion stories, testimonies to sanctifying grace, accounts of your own experiences? List three ideas you would include.

Spiritual Stepping-stones

1. Meditate on the story of the Faust painting. In what ways does it relate to your own experience of sin and salvation?

2. Sing these verses of "O for a Thousand Tongues to Sing":

> *Jesus! the name that charms our fears,*
>   *That bids our sorrows cease;*
> *'Tis music in the sinner's ears;*
>   *'Tis life, and health, and peace.*
>
> *He breaks the pow'r of canceled sin;*
>   *He sets the pris'ner free.*
> *His blood can make the foulest clean;*
>   *His blood availed for me.*
>   —Charles Wesley

3. Pray for the salvation or entire sanctification of a friend, neighbor, or family member.

Tools to Work With

1. Consider these key phrases. Ponder their meaning and use in this chapter. What is their significance?
   - "Christus Victor."
   - "The King of Kings has another move!"
   - "the first-born from the dead."
   - "not . . . a 'super' Christian [but] a true Christian."
   - "beat [our] body and make it [our] slave."
   - "in entire sanctification we permit Christ . . . to become sovereign Lord of our existence."

2. Write a letter to the author of this book. Tell him about
   - the idea or thought that meant the most to you.
   - the idea or thought that was new to you.

- the idea or thought that troubled you most and why.
- the strongest *feeling* this chapter provoked.

3. Select a verse of scripture or a phrase or sentence from your study of Rom. 6—8 or this chapter that you want, need, or ought to remember. Write it on a card and put it in your purse or wallet, on your desk, refrigerator, calendar, or dashboard—anyplace that will keep a great truth before you during the coming days.

*I have been crucified with Christ; and
it is no longer I who live, but it is Christ
who lives in me. And the life I now live
in the flesh I live by faith in the Son of God,
who loved me and gave himself for me.*
—Gal. 2:20

6

Holiness: Christ Reigning Within

GAL. 2:20 IS PAUL'S GOSPEL OF SANCTIFICATION IN all its dazzling beauty and divine complexity, set like a rare diamond between his gospel of justification (2:15-21) and the promised gift of the Spirit (3:1-14).

For Paul, as we have seen, justification and sanctification are intimately related, just as Christ's death and resurrection are two phases of one event. To die with Christ to sin is to be simultaneously raised with Him to "new life [in] the Spirit" (Rom. 7:6; see 6:1-4).

Gal. 2:20 reminds us that God's purpose in our salvation is to one end: that in some divinely mysterious way Christ may be *reincarnate in our human flesh, living out His holy life in us!* (See Rom. 8:29.)

Such is the dynamism and the potency of the gospel of holiness: Christ reigning within, ruling all our powers and gradually transforming us into His own likeness, in the power of His life-giving Spirit (see 2 Cor. 3:18; 1 Cor. 15:45).

Let us now lift up the diamond of the gospel of holiness that we find in our text and view it from its three angles. Gal. 2:20 reveals that I have

- a *sinful* self to be crucified with Christ,
- a *human* self to be disciplined in Christ, and
- a *true* self to be actualized in Christ.

A Sinful Self to Be Crucified with Christ

The Greek reads literally, "With Christ I have been cocrucified; and lives no longer I [*egō*], but lives in me Christ."

As members of Adam's fallen race we are born "curved in on ourselves," as Martin Luther said. We have a serious curvature of the heart. It is this sinful *egō* that God crucifies in the believer: the idolatrous self that dethrones God in its pride and rebellion (see Rom. 1:21-25).

▬●

**Sin is a racial fact
before it is an individual act.**

▬●

All we mortals are, without exception, members of Adam's fallen race, who because of his defection have been cut off from the sanctifying grace of the Spirit. *Deprived* of the Spirit, we are morally *depraved*. Sin is a racial fact before it is an individual act. Fallen in Adam, we inevitably "individuate" as sinners. In our own personal life *each* of us reenacts the Fall. The apostle speaks for us all when he writes, "Apart from the law sin lies dead. I was once alive apart from the law, but when the commandment came, sin revived and I died" (Rom. 7:8-10). At some point in our personal journey—we call it the age of moral accountability—each of us hears God's voice within, commanding, "Thou shalt not!" Without exception, because we are inwardly depraved, we inevitably disobey. It is thus that sin becomes *transgression*.

"Explain original sin in any way you choose," Professor Edward Ramsdell said in a university lecture; "you cannot explain it away; it is an empirical fact." Scripture says plainly, "All have sinned and fall short of the glory of God" (Rom. 3:23). That is the bad news.

Thank God, there is good news: "The saying is sure and worthy of full acceptance, that Christ Jesus came into the world to save sinners—of whom I am the foremost" (1 Tim. 1:15).

But since salvation is by grace apart from the works of the Law, and since the Law cannot produce a holy life but serves only to activate sin and turn it into transgression, and since where sin has abounded grace has all the more abounded (see Rom. 5:18-21), "What shall we say, then? Shall we go on sinning so that grace may increase?" In answer to this bogus logic the apostle resounds, "By no means! We died to sin; how can we live in it any longer?" (6:1-2, NIV). Rather than providing blanket forgiveness for all our sins "past, present, and future," justification *breaks the power of sin!*

The Old Testament guilt offering suggests a helpful illustration of justifying faith. An Israelite who had become conscious of guilt and was seeking forgiveness was to select as a guilt offering a ram without blemish from his flock and bring it to the priest. Associating himself with the victim, he must place his hand upon its head as a sign of a unity he wished to affirm and effect, while at the same time confessing the sins that had occasioned the sacrifice. As the blood flowed from the victim's throat, the sinner "died" in and with the sacrificial offering. The communion thus realized by sacrifice gave the believing Israelite access to the renewing and revitalizing forces released by contact with the altar, that is, with God, through his vicarious sacrifice.[1]

In like manner, when we come to Christ for pardon, we acknowledge that it was *our* sins that nailed *Him* to the Cross. In repentance and faith, we *appropriate* the death of Christ, His death *for* our sin thereby becoming our death *to* sin. This understanding of Christ's atoning sacrifice is the reason Paul utterly repudiates the notion that Christians can go on living in sin: "How can we who died to sin go on living in it?" (Rom. 6:2). That is to say, how can we *as Christians* go on *living* in sin, since we *as Christians* have *died* to sin?

**Jesus is now Lord,
but self would like to be
prime minister!**

A young woman who had quite a reputation for wild partying was powerfully converted in a gospel crusade. A few nights later one of her old friends called, saying, "We're having a bar-nothing party tonight. Will you go with me as my date?" to which she replied, "I'm sorry. I can't go—*I'm dead!*" There was then a click on the other end of the line. Such a death to sin, signed and sealed by baptism (see Rom. 6:3-4), is what it means to be scripturally converted. As Charles Wesley sings,

> He breaks the pow'r of canceled sin;
> He sets the pris'ner free.

Our sinful predicament, however, is deeper than the *compulsion to sinning* that God heals in conversion. Even radical conversion does not resolve the sin problem (as we may think at first). Though sin no longer *reigns*, every Christian soon discovers sin still *remains*, as an *ego-bias* rivaling Christ's reign within our hearts. Jesus is now Lord, but self would like to be prime minister!

This remaining "root" of sin is

- the presupposition of all the exhortations and prayers for holiness in the Epistles (2 Cor. 7:1; 1 Thess. 4:4-8; 5:23-24),
- the confession of all the great creeds of the Church, and
- eventually the humble confession of every justified believer endeavoring to "have the mind of Christ" and "walk as Jesus did" (1 Cor. 2:16; 1 John 2:6, NIV).

Remaining sin has been defined variously, as

- "a hard core of idolatrous self-love" (Richard S. Taylor),
- "a residue of recalcitrancy" (E. Stanley Jones),
- "the delusion of self-sovereignty" (Millard Reed),
- "my claim to my right to myself" (Oswald Chambers).

"We have met the enemy, and he is us!" comics character Pogo says. The proper way to spell *sin* is to hyphenate it: *s-I-n*—at its heart is idolatrous self-love. As the old spiritual goes,

> *Not my brother, not my sister, but it's me, O Lord,*
> *Standin' in the need of prayer.*

The remaining ego-bias that plagues the unsanctified believer demands a *deeper* death to sin—a death to *sin itself;* the death of "my claim to my right to myself." In a word, the holiness command is the imperative to *actualize my conversion.*

Paul exhorts the Roman Christians to "present" themselves to God, once and for all,[2] as those who have been brought from death to life. Returning to this gospel imperative a few verses later, he explains it in human terms because of their "natural limitations": "For just as you once presented your members as slaves to impurity and to greater and greater iniquity, *so now present your members as slaves to righteousness for sanctification*" (6:19, emphasis added). Oswald Chambers finds a mystery here—that some who were formerly such outbroken sinners choose now to be timid saints! The call is for a total abandonment of myself to God's sovereign claims upon my heart and life.

The sin that remains is clearly self-sovereignty: my determining how much of myself I will permit God to possess and purify. The call is for total self-abdication to God, *"for sanctification"*—what Wesley sometimes called "full sanctification." This sanctification is both the divine act of heart cleansing and the resulting life of holiness. The following passage makes this clear: "But now having been set free from sin, and having become slaves of God, you have your fruit to holiness, and the end, everlasting life" (Rom. 6:22, NKJV); or, "But now that you have been freed from sin and enslaved to God, the advantage you get is sanctification" (NRSV).

The complete self-giving that makes possible this full release of God's sanctifying power is beautifully foreshadowed in the self-dedication of the Hebrew slave who, not choosing to go out free in the year of jubilee, declares, "I love my master, my wife, and my children; I will not go out a free person" (Exod. 21:5). He then presents himself to his master, who pierces his ear with an awl, making him a "love slave" for life (see vv. 2-6). This is the servitude of perfect freedom.

It is in such an act of self-donation that Christ establishes His sanctifying reign in my heart, enabling me to say in all humility and praise to God: "I have been crucified with Christ; and it is no longer I who live, but it is Christ who lives in me" (Gal. 2:20).

A Human Self to Be Disciplined in Christ

Even though I have experienced a radical death to sin, and Christ now reigns in me in the power of the indwelling Spirit, my continued victory is guaranteed only as I *maintain* this vital relationship. "I have been crucified with Christ" is the perfect tense in Greek and has the force *"I have been and am now crucified with Christ."* The holy life is a moment-by-moment relationship maintained as I submit to the disciplines of the Spirit. "I say, walk by the Spirit," Paul writes later in Galatians, "and you will not carry out the desire of the flesh" (5:16, NASB).

The threat to continuing victory is posed by my *natural* self that lives on beyond the crisis of full sanctification. The King James Version catches Paul's thought when it states, "I am crucified with Christ: *nevertheless I live*" (2:20, emphasis added). The repetition of "I" and "me" throughout the text underscores the survival of the essential self beyond the crucifixion of the sinful self. It is therefore a mistake to speak of the death *of* self; in crucifixion with Christ the self dies *to* sin. "I died, and I died ungraciously," one preacher declared, "but I died only to that which made me die."

Furthermore, the holy life is a life "in the flesh": When Paul says, "The life I now live *in the flesh* [but not *according* to the flesh] I live by faith in the Son of God, who loved me and gave himself for me" (v. 20, emphasis added), he means that I live the holy life in a flesh-and-blood body, with all its passions and desires—the same kind of body, incidentally, that the Son of God assumed in the Incarnation. It was as a true man that Jesus was "tempted in every way, just as we are—yet was without sin" (Heb. 4:15, NIV). As He lived a holy life in a physical body with all its urges, drives, and desires, so may we—by the power of the same Spirit who indwelt Him! The apostle asks, "Or do you not know that your body is a temple of the Holy Spirit within you, which you have from God, and that you are not your own? For you were bought with a price; therefore glorify God in your body" (1 Cor. 6:19-20).

Elsewhere Paul writes: "If you have been raised with Christ, seek the things that are above. . . . For you have died, and your life is hidden with Christ in God. . . . Put to death, therefore, whatever in you is earthly: fornication, impurity, passion, evil desire, and greed" (Col. 3:1, 3, 5).

When Paul says in Romans, "You are not in the flesh" (8:9), he means Christians do not live "according to the flesh" (vv. 4-5, 12-13), do not have the "mind set on the flesh" (see vv. 5-7), in either self-indulgence or self-dependence (see vv. 1-7). Conversely, Paul writes, "The fruit of the Spirit is . . . self-control. . . . And those who belong to Christ Jesus have crucified the flesh with its passions and desires. If we live by the Spirit, let us also be guided by the Spirit" (Gal. 5:22-25).

"How can I live a holy life in a world like this?" a man asked the late Jack Ford, then rector of British Isles Nazarene College in Manchester, England.

"Do you believe Jesus Christ lived a holy life?" Ford countered.

"Of course," the man replied.

"The question, then, is this," Ford continued. "Will you permit Jesus Christ to live *His* holy life in *you?*"

That is the question.

The Scriptures clearly contain a doctrine of both *counteraction* and *suppression,* not of sin (which is destroyed by sanctifying grace) but of our bodily impulses that may lead to sin. In Rom. 8 Paul admonishes, "For if you are living according to the flesh, you must die; but if by the Spirit you are putting to death the deeds of the body, you will live" (v. 13, NASB). That is scriptural counteraction. Again Paul writes, "I buffet my body and make it my slave, lest possibly, after I have preached to others, I myself should be disqualified" (1 Cor. 9:27, NASB). That is scriptural suppression.

By "*sōma* (body)," a New Testament scholar writes, Paul means "the nearest equivalent of our word 'personality.'"[3] "The deeds of the body" we are commanded to "put . . . to death" are therefore our psychological as well as our physical impulses—all the mechanistic tendencies of the psyche (rationalization, projection, denial, and so on) along with the instinctual urges and drives of the body. The Spirit-filled believer remains a human ego with natural tendencies and still possesses what Freud called the "id," with its pressures and proddings. Since these impulses reside beneath the level of consciousness, they are morally neutral, but they may easily lead to sin and must therefore be controlled and subjugated by the power of the indwelling Spirit. If we "repress" them by denial, not only do we deceive ourselves, but also we become sick. By the Spirit we must "suppress" them by acknowledging them to God and permitting Him to give us victory over them (see 1 John 1:7-8).

W. E. Sangster has a helpful passage in his book *The Pure in Heart,* in which he insists that "life, as it bubbles out of the subconscious, is amoral, and should be regarded merely as instinct or 'reaction' until the conscious self identifies itself with the end desired." He continues:

> When I feel a sudden stab of jealousy, is it I?—in the very instant that I feel it? Is it I, when some surge of pride stiffens my spirit? Is it I, in the moment when some carnal appetite stirs in my flesh?
>
> Certainly, in that split second, it feels like me. . . . Is that carnality, pride, jealousy, self-pity or any other member of the dirty litter—is it mine?—mine the second that I feel it; mine whether I disown it or not?
>
> I cannot feel that it is. As a conscious moral being, it is not mine till my will makes it mine. I have an amoral nature, with race and family memories and tendencies. But, as a person, and with the help of the Holy Ghost, the animal nature can be curbed, chained, subdued, mastered. No more of it need be admitted to my moral life than fellowship with God allows. In the moment it stirs in me, trying to wrest my moral life to what I judge to be evil, it is still only temptation. If I finger it awhile and glut my imagination in it, it becomes mine, even though it has not issued in a deed, because I have taken it as my own.
>
> I will not take it as my own. I will learn from the saints how to assess it swiftly in the light of God and, seeing it to be evil, blast it with a prayer.

It was never my own. It was amoral instinct. It was only impulse bidding for moral stature. It was recognized in the white light of God in its evil tendency, and never passed the moral guard.[4]

The apostle John writes, "You are from God, little children, and have overcome them; *because greater is He who is in you than he who is in the world*" (1 John 4:4, NASB, emphasis added). Then later he adds, "And this is the victory that has overcome the world—our faith" (5:4, NASB).

A True Self to Be Actualized in Christ: "Yet Not I, but Christ"

I once understood Paul to be saying in Galatians what Jesus said in the Gospels—that if I deny myself and take up my cross daily and follow Him, I will find *self-fulfillment* (see Luke 9:23-24).

•◄━

> *Self-actualization* **is the goal of the New Age movement.**
> *Christ-actualization* **is the goal of the gospel.**

•◄━

Of course nothing is truer: the way of the Cross is indeed the way of personal fulfillment. Yet in fullest Christian perspective, self-fulfillment is only the *by-product* of crucifixion with Christ. The end God has in mind in our crucifixion with Christ is *the actualization of the divine self*—"not I, but Christ" (KJV). *Self-actualization* is the ideal of the so-called New Age movement; *Christ-actualization* is the goal of the gospel.

God's purpose in crucifying my pretentious self is simply that *Christ may become reincarnate in me* and live out *His* life of holy, loving servitude in *my* everyday, humdrum existence. Bill Bright shares with us his life in Christ:

I usually awaken with a psalm of praise on my lips, with an attitude of thanksgiving: "Oh, Lord, I thank You that I belong to You. I thank You that You live within me, and I thank You that You have forgiven my sins. I thank You that I am a child of God. Now as I begin this day, as I continue throughout the day, I thank You that You walk around in my body, love with my heart, speak with my lips, and think with my mind. I thank You that, during the course of the day, You promised to do greater things through me than You did when You were here on earth. By faith I acknowledge Your greatness, Your power, Your authority in my life, and I invite you to do anything You wish in and through me."

Then I slip out of bed on my knees, as a formal act of acknowledging His lordship.[5]

This identification with Christ is at once the secret and the simplicity of the holy life.

Have Thine own way, Lord! Have Thine own way!
Hold o'er my being absolute sway!
Fill with Thy Spirit till all shall see
Christ only, always living in me!

—Adelaide A. Pollard

Light for Your Spiritual Journey

Cornerstones

Suppose that you are going to teach this chapter to a Sunday School class. It will take two or three sessions to cover the sinful self that needs to be crucified, the natural self that needs to be disciplined, and the true self that needs to be fulfilled.

The first step in your lesson planning is to set objectives. On a separate sheet of paper, respond to these questions.

1. **What do I want my students to *know?***
   That is, what ideas, concepts, truths, and facts must they understand?

2. **What do I want my students to *feel?***
   Learning is just rote until the emotions get involved. What appreciations, longings, desires, motives, values, and so on do I hope to foster?

3. **What do I want my students to *do?***
   What *actions* do I want to result from the learning—prayer, consecration, acts of devotion, witnessing, seeking entire sanctification?

If you have a spiritual friend or prayer partner, invite him or her to work with you on this exercise.

Spiritual Stepping-stones

1. On Saving the Gazelle

"In my dream," a man said to his pastor, "I approach a cage filled with wild animals. In the front of the cage are voracious lions, tigers, and bears. In the back of the cage is a gentle, graceful, sloe-eyed gazelle. I keep trying to feed the gazelle, but the fierce animals in the front keep devouring all the food. In the end the starving gazelle grows weak and dies."

The pastoral counselor told him, "The gazelle is your true self, your best self—the part of you that is created in the image of God. The lions, tigers, and bears are perhaps greed, passion, anger, lust, and so on, that are starving that which is best in your life."

In what ways can you relate this dream to the content of this chapter? In what ways can you relate this story to your own spiritual journey? to your own life right now?

2. Christ-actualization

For many people self-fulfillment or self-realization

is the first and highest goal in life. The author says that the highest goal of the gospel is *Christ-actualization.*

Meditate on this idea. What changes would have to occur before the principle of letting Christ live His holy life again through you became a reality?

True holiness always expresses itself in unselfish service. How do *Christ-realization* and Christian service relate to each other?

John Wesley said that a person with "one grain of faith" would "spend and be spent" for others. What do you think?

If you have a spiritual friend or prayer partner, discuss and pray about this together.

3. **The Natural Self**

Some people seem to think that once you are fully sanctified, the natural self with all its psychological and physical impulses and desires will take care of itself. However, Paul and author Greathouse say that even the most holy among us must "make a slave" of the body and its physical and psychological drives and desires. What do you believe about this? What experiences on your spiritual journey shed light on this question?

4. The sinful self is to be *crucified,* but this is different from destroying your God-given *selfhood.* How important is this distinction? Is being a person (selfhood) part of the image of God in humanity?

Tools to Work With

Church services, classes, and even chapters need benedictions. Now that you have stood on the "holy ground" that this chapter reveals, write a benediction for it. To spark your thought process, we give these examples.

> *Pardon, O gracious Jesus, what we have been;*
> *With Thy holy discipline correct what we are.*

Order by Thy providence what we shall be,
And in the end crown Thine own gifts.
                                    —John Wesley
                        (personal prayer journal, unpublished)

Lord, let . . . no pride or self-seeking, no covetous-
ness or revenge, no little ends and low imagination pol-
lute my spirit . . . Let my body be a servant of my spirit
and both my body and spirit be servants of Jesus.[6]

And all of us, with unveiled faces, seeing the glory of the Lord as though reflected in a mirror, are being transformed into the same image from one degree of glory to another; for this comes from the Lord, the Spirit.

—2 Cor. 3:18

7

The Transfigured Image

WHEN MOSES DESCENDED FROM MOUNT SINAI with the two tablets of the covenant in his hand, "the skin of his face shone because he had been talking with God" (Exod. 34:29). To keep from blinding the eyes of Aaron and the Israelites, Moses put a veil on his face as he talked with them.

In comparing the Mosaic covenant to the new covenant of Christ, Paul sees a deeper purpose in Moses veiling his face: to conceal the fact that the glory that bathed his face was a *fading* glory. "We are not like Moses," Paul declares, "who veiled his face to prevent the Israelites from seeing its fading glory. . . . But all of us who are Christians have no veils on our faces, but reflect like mirrors the glory of the Lord. We are transformed in ever-increasing splendour into his own image, and this is the work of the Lord who is the Spirit" (2 Cor. 3:13, 18, PHILLIPS).

The title of this chapter is borrowed from that of a sermon by Phineas F. Bresee and expresses his conviction that the essence of sanctification is the believer's transfiguration into the likeness of Christ.

Dr. Bresee was expressing John Wesley's basic understanding of sanctification as a process in which the believer is "renewed in the image of God, 'in righteousness and true holiness.'"[1]

This process involves a series of crises in which the believer is freed from the guilt and power of sin (in conversion), from the root and inbeing of sin (in entire sanctification), and finally from the effects of sin (in glorification). But this process is all of one piece and to one end—to restore us both individually and corporately "to the measure of the full stature of Christ" (Eph. 4:13).

To be in a growing relationship with Christ is to cry,

> O to be like Thee! O to be like Thee,
> Blessed Redeemer, pure as Thou art!
> Come in Thy sweetness; come in Thy fullness.
> Stamp Thine own image deep on my heart.
>
> —Thomas O. Chisholm

Sanctification

When Adam fell, he forfeited the reflected image of God in which he had been created and was divested of the glory of God that originally had bathed his existence. But thank God,

> A second Adam to the fight,
> And to the rescue came![2]

Christ, the Second Adam, is the image of God restored (see 2 Cor. 4:4). To be in Christ is to "put on the new man, which after God is created in righteousness and true holiness" (Eph. 4:24, KJV).

Our renewal in the image of God is a progressive restoration of the likeness and glory of God. To the Colossians, Paul wrote, "You have stripped off the old self with its practices and have clothed yourselves with the new self, which is being renewed in knowledge according to the image of its creator" (3:9-10). Indeed, we "are being changed into his likeness from one degree of glory to another; . . . from the Lord who is the [life-giving] Spirit" (2 Cor. 3:18, RSV; see 1 Cor. 15:45).

> *That I, a child of hell,*
> *Should in His image shine!*
> *The Comforter has come!*
> —Frank Bottome

At the same time, it is a fact that all of us who are Christians, even the truly sanctified, "fall short of the glory of God" (Rom. 3:23); the full restoration of that glory awaits Christ's second advent. In that event He will consummate our salvation: "He will transform the body of our humiliation that it may be conformed to the body of his glory" (Phil. 3:21).

Even so, "if we walk in the light as he himself is in the light" (1 John 1:7), "Christ, who is the image of God" (2 Cor. 4:4), gradually transfigures us into His likeness, although, like Moses, we are unaware this change is taking place (see Exod. 34:29). But one day, all praise to His grace, "we *will* be like him, for we will see him as he is" (1 John 3:2, emphasis added).

The glory of God shines into our hearts, and our transformation begins.

Initial Sanctification

Our transfiguration begins in conversion. This is clear from what Paul writes in 2 Corinthians: "The light of the gospel of the glory of Christ, who is the image of God" is "veiled to those who are perishing," their eyes "blinded" by "the god of this world." But Paul can say of himself and of all of us who believe, "The God who said, 'Let light shine out of darkness,' . . . has shone in our hearts to give the light of the knowledge of the glory of God in the face of Jesus Christ" (4:4, 3, 6).

For Paul, this miracle of transformation began when the risen Christ confronted him on the Damascus road.

For us, transformation into Christlikeness begins when in repentance and faith we encounter the crucified, resurrected Jesus. In that moment, "the glory of God in the face of Jesus Christ" shines into our hearts and begins our transfiguration into His likeness.

But this metamorphosis is no mere private matter. We must publicly confess our faith and by baptism identify ourselves with Christ's Body. It must always be said of us, as of all New Testament Christians, "As many of you as were baptized into Christ have clothed yourselves with Christ," in whose Body "there is no longer Jew or Greek, there is no longer slave or free, there is no longer male and female; for all of you are one in Christ Jesus" (Gal. 3:27-28).

**Into his love comes fear.
Into his faith comes doubt.
Into his humility comes pride.**

Entire Sanctification

"By justification," says John Wesley, "we are saved from the guilt of sin, and restored to the favour of God; by sanctification we are saved from the power and root of sin, and *restored to the image of God*" (emphasis added).[3]

By the image of God, Wesley understands "the holy, humble, gentle, patient love of God and man." This love "begins the moment we are justified," as "all experience, as well as Scripture, show."[4]

But in the newly converted, this love is "mingled with doubts or fears" and "mixed" with remaining sinful self-love.[5] In the glow of newfound faith, young Christians may be blissfully unaware of remaining sin. But sooner or later they discover a lurking self-idolatry rivaling Christ's control and disturbing their peace and joy. But Dr. Bresee points out that there is trouble ahead: "There is opposition to this new life in his own being; . . . though he loves God he does not love Him with all his heart, and . . . self intrudes. Into his love comes fear. Into his faith comes doubt. Into his humility comes pride. Into his devotement comes ambition and self-seeking. There is struggle in his breast. He looks up into the pure Spirit of Jesus by the light of the Holy Ghost and is overwhelmed."[6]

But blessed is the Christian who comes to this conviction of remaining sin and groans for deliverance. "Blessed are those who mourn," says Jesus, "for they will be comforted" (Matt. 5:4). For such a one, says Wesley, God is ready "to fulfil that promise which he made first to his ancient people, and in them to the Israel of God in all ages: 'I will circumcise thy heart, and the heart of thy seed, to love the Lord thy God with *all* thy heart, and with *all* thy soul'" (emphases added; see Deut. 30:6, KJV).[7]

The promise of perfect love is the promise of "pure love"—that is, of love *unmixed* with idolatrous self-love. In the deeper crisis of entire sanctification, the heart is purified from sinful self-love. Wesley explains, "Till this universal change was wrought in his soul, all his holiness was *mixed*. . . . His whole soul is now consistent with itself. . . . There is no mixture of any contrary affections: All is peace and harmony [within]."[8]

But after this inward change, Wesley continues, "he still grows in grace, in the knowledge of Christ, in the love and image of God; and will do so, not only till death, but to all eternity."[9]

In entire sanctification, Wesley concludes, "the heart is cleansed from all sin, and filled with pure love to God and man. But even that love increases more and more, till we 'grow up in all things into Him that is our Head;' till we attain 'the measure of the stature of the fulness of Christ.'"[10]

Final Sanctification

A caveat must here be entered. Even though the cry of my heart is that of Paul's—"I want to know Christ and the power of his resurrection," I must always confess with him, "Not that I have already obtained this or have already reached the goal; . . . but this one thing I do: forgetting what lies behind and straining forward to what lies ahead, I press on toward the goal for the prize of the heavenly call of God in Christ Jesus" (Phil. 3:10, 12-14). In all honesty and humility I daily confess,

> *I'm a person God is making,*
> *Like a statue God is shaping;*
> *God is changing me, correcting,*
> *God's intent on my perfecting.*

But I am not yet perfected!

Paul the apostle and every saint of God, however ripe and mature, freely acknowledge with E. Stanley Jones that we are but "Christians *in the making.*"

I remember one of the most mature and Christlike saints I have ever known saying to me, "Brother Greathouse, sometimes I feel so *earthy!*" Sometimes indeed we feel so dull when we should be keen and bright. Sometimes we feel so depressed when we should feel happy. Sometimes we act so human when we yearn to be Christlike. Remember: we still have unredeemed bodies.

Yet all this is by divine design. "If Christianity be not altogether restless eschatology," Karl Barth incisively writes, "there remains in it no relationship whatever to Christ."[11] It is "the sufferings of this present time"—between Pentecost and the Parousia (see Rom. 8:18-23)—that keeps us prayerful and Christ-dependent.

We are no longer what we once were, but we are not yet what we *shall* be—when Christ returns to redeem our bodies and complete our sanctification. Listen to Paul as he pens the following passage to the Corinthians:

> Behold, I tell you a mystery: We shall not all sleep, but we shall all be changed—in a moment, in the twinkling of an eye, at the last trumpet. . . . We shall be changed. . . . Then shall be brought to pass the saying that is written: *"Death is swallowed up in victory. O Death, where is your sting? O Hades, where is your victory?"*
>
> The sting of death is sin, and the strength of sin is the law. But thanks be to God, who gives us the victory through our Lord Jesus Christ *(1 Cor. 15:51-52, 54-57, NKJV).*

It was *"in this hope"*—the hope of glorification—that with Christ "we were saved" (Rom. 8:24, RSV).

Light for Your Spiritual Journey

Cornerstones

Finish these sentences as a review of the content of this chapter.

● Sanctification is _____

_____

_____

● Initial sanctification is _____

_____

_____

● Entire sanctification is _____

_____

_____

● Final sanctification is _____

_____

_____

Spiritual Stepping-stones

"Top 10" lists are popular these days. Make your own top-10 list of the words, phrases, or ideas in this chapter that bring you the most inspiration, comfort, encouragement, or hope. For example, "Love unmixed with idolatrous self-love" would be somewhere in my top 10. Fill in your own selections, saving the most meaningful for the "1" position.

10 _____

9 _____

8 _____

7 _____

6 _____

5 _____

4 _____

3 _____

2 _____

1 _____

Tools to Work With

Here are two stanzas of a Charles Wesley hymn. In my 1849 edition of *Hymns for the Use of the People Called Methodists* it is hymn No. 408. It has no title. Your assignment, should you choose to accept it, is to add one verse of your own. It can become the first, second, or last verse. Make it reflect your own heartfelt needs or praise. The second part of the assignment is to give the hymn a title.

> *He wills that I should holy be;*
> *That holiness I long to feel;*
> *That full divine conformity*
> *To all my Saviour's righteous will.*

Come, Saviour, come, and make me whole;
Entirely all my sins remove;
To perfect health restore my soul,
To perfect holiness and love.

Your verse: _____

_____

_____

_____

Your title: _____

May the God of peace himself
sanctify you entirely;
and may your spirit and soul and body
be kept sound and blameless
at the coming of our Lord Jesus Christ.
The one who calls you is faithful,
and he will do this.

—1 Thess. 5:23-24

8

A Prayer for Entire Sanctification

IN EXAMINING THE FOUNDATIONS FOR THE HOLY life, no book is more important than 1 Thessalonians, generally regarded by many scholars as the earliest of Paul's letters (about A.D. 50) and therefore the oldest piece of Christian literature in existence.

Most significantly, 1 Thessalonians contains a higher density of specific holiness terms than any other Pauline letter, with a percentage twice the average of the entire body of his letters. Paul's benedictory prayer in 5:23-24, the only explicit reference to *entire* sanctification in his writings, summarizes the apostle's concerns in the letter and witnesses to the centrality of holiness in First Thessalonians.[1]

As a young Christian, I read the five brief chapters of 1 Thessalonians in one sitting for my evening devotions. That evening I found a narrative account of Christian holiness that squared with what I had been taught as a new Nazarene, an understanding that has been a lodestar in my theology ever since. Before reading further, however, consult 1 Thessalonians for yourself. Take a few minutes and read the five short chapters; then with your Bible open before you, consider the outline that follows "to see whether these things [are] so" (Acts 17:11).

1. The Thessalonians Were True Believers (1:1—2:16)

Everything Paul says about his Thessalonian converts witnesses to their genuine conversion to Christianity. They beautifully exemplified faith, hope, and love, evidence of their true Christian experience (1:3)—"a moral life marked by faithfulness to God, hopeful expectation of final salvation, and fraternal love in the meantime."[2]

The Thessalonians' election to salvation was clearly demonstrated. The gospel had come to them "not in word only, but also in power and in the Holy Spirit and with full conviction" (vv. 4-5). "In spite of persecution" they had "received the word with joy inspired by the Holy Spirit," thereby becoming "an example to all the believers" of the region (vv. 6-7). They had "turned to God from idols, to serve a living and true God, and to wait for his Son from heaven" (vv. 9-10).

The second chapter continues the story of their faith and of the loving relationship that existed between them and the apostle. It likens the Thessalonian church to "the churches of God in Christ Jesus . . . in Judea," in that these believers had "suffered the same things from [their] own compatriots" that the churches in Judea had suffered from the "Jews, who killed both the Lord Jesus and the prophets" (2:14-15).

2. The Thessalonians' Faith Had Stood the Test of Severe Persecution (2:17—3:9)

Paul's preaching at Thessalonica had stirred up unbelieving Jews who "formed a mob and set the city in an uproar. . . . That very night the believers sent Paul and Silas off to Beroea" (Acts 17:5, 10; see vv. 1-10). In this way Paul was forced to leave—"in person, not in heart" (1 Thess. 2:17)—the newly converted pagans in Thessalonica. "We longed with great eagerness to see you face to face," Paul writes, ". . . but Satan blocked our way. For what is our hope or joy or crown of boasting before our Lord Jesus at his coming? Is it not you? Yes, you are our glory and joy!" (vv. 17-20).

When he could bear it no longer, Paul dispatched Timothy from Athens (where he had gone from Berea) to "strengthen and encourage" (3:2) the Thessalonians, lest they be "shaken by these persecutions" (v. 3), and his labor among them be proven to have "been in vain" (v. 5).

"But Timothy has just now come to us from you," Paul continues, "and has brought us the good news of your faith and love. . . . For we now live, if you continue to stand firm in the Lord" (vv. 6, 8). The encouraging report gave the apostle an occasion of rejoicing before God (vv. 6, 8-9).

3. There Was a Remaining Lack in the Thessalonians' Faith (3:10—4:12)

Despite their triumphant endurance and evident love, we now read, Paul was "night and day praying exceedingly" for the Thessalonians, "that [he] may see [them] and *perfect* [*supply*—NIV, RSV] what [was] lacking in [their] faith" (3:10, NKJV, emphasis added). The Greek verb in the latter clause comes from a root that means "rendering complete," "fitting together," or "reconciling factions." It is used here to mean the supplying of what is missing for the full discharge of the functions for which these believers were designed of God (cf. Eph. 4:12).[3]

Paul's prayer to see the Thessalonians "face to face" has theological significance. The apostolic presence is commonly linked with the desire to perfect a church's faith (cf. Rom. 1:11).[4] Having been abruptly removed from Thessalonica, the apostle now longs to return *in person* and *perfect* their inadequate faith and experience.

The imperfection of the Thessalonians was in two interrelated areas: in their *love* and in their *holiness* (3:11—4:12). Both were genuine, but their love needed to be perfected and their holiness completed.

***

Their imperfections had to do with love and holiness.

***

In addressing these remaining deficiencies, the apostle's approach is noticeably positive. His attitude is clearly revealed in his prayer for the church: "Now may our God and Father himself and our Lord Jesus Christ direct our way to you. *And may the Lord make you increase and abound in love* for one another and for all, just as we abound in love for you. *And may he so strengthen your hearts in holiness* that you may be blameless before our God and Father at the coming of our Lord Jesus with all his saints" (3:11-13, emphases added). This prayer suggests clearly that abounding love and blamelessness in holiness are two aspects of one whole.

A look at 4:9-12 shows again Paul's positive approach to their need for a fullness of love: "Now concerning love of the brothers and sisters, you do not need to have anyone write to you," he explains, *"for you yourselves have been taught by God to love one another; and indeed you do love. . . .* But we urge you, beloved, *to do so more and more"* (4:9-10, emphases added; see Eph. 3:14-19).

With respect to their holiness, the apostle takes the same approach when he writes, "Finally, brothers and sisters, we ask and urge you in the Lord Jesus that, as you have learned from us how you ought to live and please God *(as, in fact, you are doing), you should do so more and more*" (4:1, emphasis added). Then specific injunctions follow that spell out what it means to be holy in heart and life, in a pagan culture rife with immorality and seething with lustful passion. Lyons explains, "Paul proceeds from the theological assumption that the character of Christians is fundamentally different from that of pagans because of the character of their God. Pagans behave as they do because they 'do not know God' (4:5; cf. 2 Thess. 1:8; Gal. 4:9). Paul characterizes his moral teaching to the Thessalonians as an exhortation to 'lead a life worthy of God, who calls you into his own kingdom and glory'" (2:12).[5]

"This is the will of God," Paul urges, "your sanctification: that you abstain from unchastity" (4:3, RSV). The apostle's instruction was not "Do as I *say*," but "Do as I *do.*" Earlier in the letter he had reminded them: "You are witnesses, and God also, how pure, upright, and blameless our conduct was toward you believers" (2:10; see 1:5-6; 2:3-4; 2 Cor. 1:12). The apostle *incarnated* the gospel he preached, and he expected his converts to imitate him in leading "a life worthy of God, who calls you into his own kingdom and glory" (2:12)—a life of transparent holiness.[6]

God did not call the Thessalonians "to impurity but in holiness" (4:7). The Greek noun for "holiness" here (*hagiasmos,* as in verses 3 and 7) defines a *process* of sanctification: "a divine activity which is manifest in concrete activity on the part of the faithful."[7] The idea conveyed is that the Thessalonians had been called of God in the *realm of* holiness. Therefore, anyone who rejects the call to *entire* sanctification "rejects not human authority but God, who also gives his Holy Spirit to you," paraphrased by J. B. Phillips, "It is not for nothing that the Spirit God gives us is called the *Holy* Spirit" (v. 8). True holiness is not a human dogma; it is the work of the sanctifying Spirit that we reject at the danger of our own loss. And holiness must embrace the sexual realm of our experience. Although self-idolatry is the *root* of sin, sexual immorality is its first and most obvious *fruit* (see Rom. 1:21-27; Gal. 5:19). The holy life is a life of moral purity.

4. The Apostle Concludes with a Prayer for the Thessalonians' *Entire* Sanctification

"May the God of peace himself sanctify you entirely; and may your spirit and soul and body be kept sound and blameless at the coming of our Lord Jesus Christ. The one who calls you is faithful, and he will do this" (5:23-24).

This prayer is clearly "the summit of the epistle." It repeats Paul's "prayer-wish" in 3:9-13 and pulls together all the vital elements of his instructions in 4:1 through 5:22, bringing to a climax the entire Epistle. Within this prayer we see a conscious and deliberate summary of all that has come before, in a broad and comprehensive benediction.[8]

This benedictory prayer is threefold, revealing the *subject*, the *scope*, and the *surety* of entire sanctification.

The Subject

"The emphasis is on God *himself* as the acting subject," says Spross.[9] While the Holy Spirit is the active Agent in effecting sanctification (see 2 Thess. 2:13), He does not operate without human cooperation, as Paul's exhortations to holy living clearly imply. God's call to holiness can be rejected (see 1 Thess. 4:8). The Spirit purifies, motivates, and enables holy living, but our personal participation is always presupposed.[10] As Augustine and others have said, "Without God we cannot; without us God will not."

While putting ourselves at God's disposal is essential to true sanctification (see Rom. 6:13, 19), only "the God of peace himself" (1 Thess. 5:23) can accomplish our entire sanctification. For Paul the Jew, the peace God gives is *shalom,* true well-being, wholeness, and blessedness. Here it also means "final salvation, which is the ultimate blessing which the Lord gives to his people."[11]

⊷

Without God we cannot; without us God will not.

⊷

Paul employs the aorist tense here, a usage that lends itself to the view that sanctification comes to completion within a process that begins at conversion and continues to the return of Christ. One scholar goes so far as to suggest that the verb here "must mean 'conform to the nature of God.' This certainly includes moral perfection without being limited to it."[12] God himself sanctifies us in our consecration, in our total separation from sin, and in our self-abandonment to His working within us. Leon Morris points out that "while there is a human element, in that a man must yield himself up to God (see 4:4), yet the primary thing is the power of God which enables this to be made good."[13]

The Scope

"May the God of peace himself sanctify you *entirely*" (1 Thess. 5:23, emphasis added). The compound adverb *holoteleis,* found only here in the New Testament, literally means "wholly and perfectly." "Carrying the sense of fullness, completeness, and totality," Dan Spross explains, "the sanctification prayed for is an entire sanctification."[14] The NIV "through and through" follows Luther's German *durch und durch.* Paul's prayer is for the Thessalonians' *total* moral and spiritual renovation, the concern of Charles Wesley's prayer when he wrote,

> *Finish then Thy new creation;*
> *Pure and spotless let us be.*

Let us see Thy great salvation,
Perfectly restored in Thee.

Other scholars find a further implication in the adverb. Leon Morris observes, "The point is that the word is a compound of which the first part has the meaning 'wholly.' If the second part is to have its proper significance we need something to bring out the thought of reaching one's proper end, the end for which one was made."[15] Then we must ask, "What is the proper end for which we were made?" Adam Clarke says to this very point, "As God requires every man to love him with all the heart, soul, mind, and strength, and his neighbour as himself; then he is a perfect man that does so; *he answers to the end for which God made him*" (emphasis added).[16] Entire sanctification is to the end or purpose of perfect love.[17]

Paul's prayer for the Thessalonians' sanctification includes the further petition for their preservation in holiness. "And may your spirit and soul and body be kept sound [or 'complete,' margin] and blameless at the coming of our Lord Jesus Christ" (5:23). The majority of interpreters take the terms "spirit and soul and body" in a collective sense, signifying the totality of the human personality. Even though the apostle is using Greek terms, he is thinking as a Hebrew, like our Lord when He commanded that we love God with all our heart and soul and mind (see Matt. 22:37)—that is, with our entire being. Entire sanctification is moral and spiritual *wholeness*, spiritual health restored and preserved by the power of God.

Thank God, we may be kept "blameless at the coming of our Lord Jesus Christ" (5:23). Blamelessness is not to be taken as something to be reserved for the moment of Christ's appearing. The word translated "kept" (*tērētheiē*) has a double connotation, including not only the idea of conservation and preservation, but also the idea of shielding, defending, and protecting. According to Gordon Pitts Wiles, the term "implies the continuation of that which already exists—so their present sanctification will be maintained at the parousia. The prayer that they may be kept wholly blameless at the parousia therefore implies their present sanctification as well."[18] In this vein, Ernest Best writes: "Holiness, of course, will not come suddenly into existence then unless they are now already 'holy' and seeking holiness. If believers are preserved in the Day of Judgment, this will imply preservation until then."[19]

—

How much religion must I have?

—

"How much religion must I have?" someone asked. Answer: "Enough to be comfortable at the thought that Christ may come at any moment." The truly sanctified pray with John the revelator, "Amen. Come, Lord Jesus!" (Rev. 22:20).

The Surety

"The one who calls you is faithful, and he will do this" (1 Thess. 5:24). Like justifying faith, sanctifying faith gives "glory to God; . . . being fully persuaded that, what he had promised, he was able also to perform" (Rom. 4:20-21, KJV).

"But what is that faith whereby we are sanctified—saved from sin and perfected in love?" John Wesley asks. He answers,

> It is a divine evidence and conviction, First, that God hath promised it in the Holy Scripture. Till we are thoroughly satisfied of this, there is no moving one step further. And one would imagine there needed not one word more to satisfy a reasonable man of this, than the ancient promise, "Then will I circumcise thy heart, and the heart of thy seed, to love the Lord thy God with all thy heart, and with all thy soul. . . ." How clearly does this express the being perfected in love!—how strongly imply the be-

ing saved from all sin! For as long as love fills up the whole heart what room is there for sin therein?

It is a divine evidence and conviction, Secondly, that what God hath promised He is able to perform. Admitting, therefore, that "with men it is impossible," yet this creates no difficulty in the case, seeing "with God all things are possible." . . . If God speaks, it shall be done. . . .

It is, Thirdly, a divine evidence and conviction that He is able and willing to do it now. And why not? Is not a moment to Him the same as a thousand years? He cannot want more time to accomplish whatever is His will. And He cannot want or stay for any more *worthiness* or *fitness* in the persons He is pleased to honour. We may therefore boldly say, at any point of time, "Now is the day of salvation!" "Today, if ye will hear His voice, harden not your hearts!" . . .

To this confidence, that God is both able and willing to sanctify us now, there needs to be added only one thing more, a divine evidence and conviction that He *doeth* it. In that hour it is done. . . . The believer then experiences the deep meaning of those solemn words, "If we walk in the light as He is in the light, we have fellowship one with another, and the blood of Jesus Christ His Son cleanseth from all sin."[20]

While at Nazarene Theological Seminary in Kansas City, I was invited to meet with ministers of Kirksville, Missouri, to engage in an exegesis of Romans, chapters 6 through 8. Fifteen or 16 ministers representing major denominations were present, along with the Roman Catholic priest and the Nazarene and Assembly of God pastors. We met at a small white country church outside the city. Sitting around a large table, we worked through chapters 6 and 7 before lunch. After lunch we spent more than an hour in chapter 8. I was deeply impressed by the unity of understanding that seemed to prevail as we simply endeavored to let the apostle speak to us from this Epistle. By midafternoon we had come to the definitive statement of the chapter: "Those who are in the flesh cannot please God. But you are not in the flesh, you are in the Spirit, if in fact the Spirit of God [really] dwells in you" (vv. 8-9, RSV, emphasis added). I emphasized that when Paul wrote, "You are not in the flesh, you are in the Spirit," he was not writing to the saints in heaven, but to the saints in Rome!

I then felt led to share my own witness to the Spirit's sanctifying grace. When I concluded, the Baptist pastor, sitting in a cane-bottomed chair next to me, asked, "But how can you *know* when you are truly sanctified?" I was about to respond when the Roman Catholic priest, sitting on a high stool next to his Protestant brother, interrupted. Putting his hand on the latter's bald head, he said kindly, "The day came when, looking into the mirror as you shaved, you said to yourself, 'Why, I'm bald-headed!' So there comes that moment when, yielded to God in full obedience, we exclaim to ourselves, *'It's done!'*"

"But how do you know that you are sanctified, saved from your inbred corruption?" Wesley asks. He answers, "We know it by the witness and by the fruit of the Spirit."[21] The fruit corroborates the witness. Entire sanctification is more than an experience; it is a life-changing work of God's grace that purifies the heart from its self-idolatry, perfects it in the love of God and neighbor, and accelerates the believer's growth in Christlikeness. As it was God's promise to entirely sanctify the Thessalonians, it is also His promise to do this for us today! *"The one who calls you is faithful, and he will do this"* (1 Thess. 5:24, emphasis added).

> *O for a heart to praise my God,*
> *A heart from sin set free,*
> *A heart that always feels Thy blood*
> *So freely shed for me.*
>
> *A heart resigned, submissive, meek,*
> *My great Redeemer's throne,*
> *Where only Christ is heard to speak,*
> *Where Jesus reigns alone.*

O for a lowly, contrite heart,
    Believing, true, and clean,
Which neither life nor death can part
    From Him that dwells within.

A heart in ev'ry thought renewed
    And full of love divine,
Perfect and right and pure and good—
    A copy, Lord, of Thine.

—Charles Wesley

Light for Your Spiritual Journey

Cornerstones

Getting a Sense of Being There

Step into the shoes of a member of the house church of Christians in Thessalonica. You come home from work exhausted. You don't know if you have enough energy to make it to church tonight. But then an excited church member tells you, "There's a letter from Paul! You don't want to miss this meeting. Our pastor is going to read it to the whole group!"

Paul—a letter from Paul! Suddenly your feet don't ache anymore. At 7 P.M. sharp you and your family are at the meeting sitting right up front. What will Paul have to say?

1. How would you react when you hear Paul's words commending your faith, love, steadfastness in persecution, and good example? What would you

- **think?** _____
- **feel?** _____
- **say?** _____
- **do?** _____

2. How would you react when the pastor reads the
statements of love and endearment? When the pastor
reads phrases like "a nurse tenderly caring for her own
children," "So deeply do we care," "share . . . our own
selves," or "you have become very dear to us" (1 Thess.
2:7-8), what would you

- **think?** _____
- **feel?** _____
- **say?** _____
- **do?** _____

3. When the reader shares Paul's intention to perfect what was *"lacking* in your faith" (3:10, emphasis
added), what would you

- **think?** _____
- **feel?** _____
- **say?** _____
- **do?** _____

4. When you hear that God's will for you (and the
whole congregation) was sanctification and sexual purity (4:3), what would you

- **think?** _____
- **feel?** _____
- **say?** _____
- **do?** _____

5. When the pastor reads the prayer that God
would entirely sanctify you (5:23-24), what would you

- **think?** _____
- **feel?** _____
- **say?** _____
- **do?** _____

Stepping-stones to Sanctifying Grace

List here the four steps a Christian should take to receive sanctifying grace. Read again the extended quote from John Wesley near the end of this chapter. The four stepping-stones are

1. _____

2. _____

3. _____

4. _____

Are you willing to follow the leading of the Spirit and take those steps now?

Tools to Work With

Some things to remember:

• Your conversion experience, being born again, was a mighty act of grace. It changed your life—just as it did for the Thessalonians whose faith, love, work, and steadfastness were commendable. The new birth is not a mere preamble to sanctification. Take time right now to praise God for saving grace.

• The fact that God calls you to a deeper experience of purity and obedience should not bring you into despair. Thanking God for what He has already done for you, yield yourself to Him. He loves you and wants only the best for you.

• Every Christian generation has produced two kinds of Christians—the ordinary garden variety who muddle along with about as much failure as victory, but also those who have found the deeper life, the sanctified life. They have discovered a deeper experience of Christlikeness. With it comes fulfillment, joys, and satisfaction that some Christians only dream of.

The hunger of your soul tells you which group you want to be a part of. Don't let the "maddening maze of things" like car pools, night classes, music lessons, soccer practice, and television cause the vision to fade. He is calling you. And if He calls, He will be faithful to give to you that which He has promised. Put all your trust in Him. He will speak the second time, "Be thou clean."

God is love, and those who abide in love
abide in God, and God abides in them. Love
has been perfected among us in this: that we
may have boldness on the day of judgment,
because as he is, so are we in this world.
There is no fear in love, but perfect love casts
out fear; for fear has to do with punishment,
and whoever fears has not reached perfection
in love. We love because he first loved us.
—1 John 4:16-19

9

Love Made Perfect

IN THE OLD TESTAMENT, GOD IS REVEALED AS *holy*—separate from all He has created, bathed in a glory that is His alone, "of purer eyes than to behold evil" (Hab. 1:13, NKJV). The prophet Isaiah's Temple experience powerfully illustrates God's holiness. As the veil of sense receded, Isaiah caught a glimpse of the Lord "high and lifted up" and heard the seraphim chanting,

Holy, holy, holy is the LORD of hosts;

The whole earth is full of His glory!

The vision utterly humbled the prophet, who cried out,

Woe is me, for I am undone!

Because I am a man of unclean lips,
And I dwell in the midst of a people of unclean lips;
For my eyes have seen the King,
The LORD of hosts.

—Isa. 6:1, 3, 5, NKJV

Holy Love

In the New Testament, the holy God is revealed as *love*. First John 4 summarizes the Christian revelation of God as love; this chapter is the New Testament equivalent of Isa. 6, which encapsulates God's revelation as holy. The God who first disclosed himself as "the Holy One of Israel" has come to us in Christ and made himself known as love—*holy love* (see Isa. 1:4; 10:17; 12:6; et al.). This dual revelation of God is foundational to all right thinking concerning God and His redemptive purposes for us mortals.

But what does John *mean* by declaring that "God is love"? Our English word *love* offers no clues whatsoever. "Love" is a chameleon word that takes on the color of whatever it is associated with. In William Sangster's words, it covers everything from "puppy love" (which often leads to a dog's life!) to the majestic love of God, which moved Him to offer up Christ to be the Sacrifice for the sins of the world. To say in English "God is love" is to utter a nonidea.

You are no doubt aware that in the Greek language the situation is different. In that tongue there are at least four definitive words to express the various kinds of loves we may experience.[1]

Two Greek words are sufficient to consider in order to clarify what John is saying here in this chapter—*erōs* (human love) and *agapē* (divine love).[2] *Erōs* is *need* love; *agapē* is *gift* love. To understand this distinction is absolutely essential to right thinking about God and human salvation, and particularly about "love made perfect."

Erōs is the love of desire arising from the incompleteness of finite personality. It is the love that desires the other—desires to possess and be united with the other—and in that union with and possession of the other, *erōs* finds fulfillment.

The Greeks had several myths concerning *erōs*. According to one, we mortals were originally composite beings, male and female in one. But we disturbed the gods, who in their anger hurled down thunderbolts on us and separated us. Ever since then, one half has been looking for the other.[3] Thus, in its essential nature *erōs* was a noble, pure concept.[4]

The Bible tells us that *erōs* was God's own idea and creation. In the beginning He created us "male and female" (Gen. 1:27). The Lord said, "It is not good that the man should be alone" (2:18). So God formed Eve as the man's partner. We read in Genesis, "Therefore a man leaves his father and his mother and clings to his wife, and they become one flesh" (v. 24).[5] But notice that the woman was to be his *wife*; *erōs* is intended by the Creator to be enjoyed in *marriage*, not indulged promiscuously as in our increasingly pagan culture.

When enjoyed according to the divine intention—sanctified by the commitment and fidelity of marriage—*erōs* is one of the most precious gifts God has bestowed on humanity.[6] Nevertheless, one's spouse cannot fulfill *all* one's needs, and to expect total human fulfillment in marriage is to fall into either idolatry (the worship of the creature rather than the Creator) or frustration and confusion, since human love can never fulfill the deepest yearnings of the human soul.

Understanding the need of the finite for the infinite, the Greeks spoke of the *heavenly erōs*: the soul's desire for the true, the good, the beautiful—for *God*. Augustine gave this truth classic expression when he confessed, "Thou madest us for Thyself, and our heart is restless, until it repose in Thee."[7]

The songwriter expressed a similar idea:

> *All my lifelong I had panted*
> > *For a drink from some cool spring*
> *That I hoped would quench the burning*
> > *Of the thirst I felt within.*
>
> *Feeding on the husks around me*
> > *Till my strength was almost gone,*
> *Longed my soul for something better,*
> > *Only still to hunger on.*
>
> *Hallelujah! I have found Him—*
> > *Whom my soul so long has craved!*
> *Jesus satisfies my longings;*
> > *Through His blood I now am saved.*
>
> —Clara T. Williams

Erōs is our human love for God, which finds its true completement only in Christ, the Water and the Bread of Life.

—

Jesus came to rescue us from the quicksand of our depravity, wash us from our iniquity, and refashion us in His own image.

—

As sublime and beautiful as is the concept of *erōs*, it is not the New Testament idea of love. The Christian term for love is *agapē*—not our love for God, but *God's love for us!* John writes, "In this is love *[agapē]*, not that we loved God but that he loved us and sent his Son to be the atoning sacrifice for our sins. . . . So we have known and believe the love that God has for us. . . . We love [God and others] because he first loved us" (1 John 4:10, 16, 19).[8] Here we are at the very core of the gospel—God's prior, unconditional, universal love for us.

Erōs is our love ascending to God; *agapē* is God's love descending to us.

Agapē is God's own love come down to us from heaven, clothing itself in Jesus the Christ, entering fully into our human situation (only sin excepted).

Incarnate in Christ, and with a cross upon its back, *Agapē* stumbled out to a hill called Calvary and poured itself out there as "the atoning sacrifice for our sins." This Christ did to break down all the barriers we mortals had erected between ourselves and the holy God, through the free pardon of all our sins; to lift us from the quicksand of our depravity and wash us from our iniquity, thereby restoring us to communion with our Creator and through it all refashioning us in His very image and likeness!

Saved by Love

To *"know and rely on the love God has for us"* (1 John 4:16, NIV, emphasis added) is to be saved. Charles Haddon Spurgeon, for many years pastor of Metropolitan Tabernacle in London, was as a young man religiously confused. "I suppose I would have remained confused," he said, "except for a blizzard that came to London one Sunday morning." Endeavoring to find his way to a certain church but blinded by the snow, Spurgeon eventually found an open door off the sidewalk. Entering the door, he found a dozen or so brave souls gathered in a small Primitive Methodist chapel. Spurgeon slipped into a pew under the balcony.

As the people waited, it soon became apparent their pastor had been snowbound. After some minutes one of the lay members arose, Bible in hand, and mounted the pulpit. He gave out for his text Isa. 45:22: "Look unto me, and be ye saved, all the ends of the earth" (KJV). "This is Jesus speaking," the good man began, "Jesus on the Cross." Continuing, he quoted John: "As Moses lifted up the serpent in the wilderness, even so must the Son of man be lifted up: that whosoever believeth in him should not perish, but have eternal life" (John 3:14-15, KJV). After about 10 minutes, Spurgeon said, the man had come to "the end of his tether." He concluded his remarks in these words: "It don't take no college education to be saved! You don't even have to raise your foot! It's simply *look to Jesus—and live!*"

"Then," Spurgeon said, "focusing on me there under the balcony, he said, 'Young man, you look *miserable!* You will *always* be miserable unless you look to Jesus. Young man, look to Jesus. Look to Jesus *now!*"

"I *did* look," Spurgeon testified, "and the burden of sin rolled from my shoulders as God's peace filled my heart! In that moment I could have stood and sung with the saintliest of them,

> There is a fountain filled with blood
> Drawn from Immanuel's veins;
> And sinners, plunged beneath that flood,
> Lose all their guilty stains."
>
> —William Cowper

But as glorious as it is to be forgiven, the miracle wrought by faith is even greater. To be pardoned from sin is also to be "born of God" and to begin to participate in *agapē.* As John says, "Everyone who loves is born of God and knows God. . . . If we love one another, God lives in us, and his love is perfected in us" (1 John 4:7, 12).

Two truths seem clear: (1) to be born of God is to receive His love, and (2) to truly love one another as Jesus commanded is to have "the love of God perfected" (1 John 2:5, KJV; see Matt. 22:34-40; John 13:34-35).

Perfect Love

Obviously, there are *degrees* of *agapē,* as this passage implies: "Love has been *perfected* among us in this: that we may have boldness on the day of judgment, because as he is, so are we in this world. There is no fear in love, but *perfect love* casts out fear . . . and whoever fears has not reached *perfection in love*" (1 John 4:17-18, emphases added).

All the Greek verbs and nouns in this passage pertaining to perfection derive from the root *telos,* meaning "end," "goal," "purpose." *Agapē* reaches its divinely intended goal *when it is incarnate in us*—when of us it can be said, "As he is, so are we in this world" (v. 17). The pronoun "he" here is literally "that one," used five times in this Epistle to refer to Christ. The apostle is therefore saying, "As *Christ* is, so are we in this world." *Agapē* has reached "perfection" (NEB)—"is made complete" (NIV)—when it has refashioned us in Christlikeness. The love of God *reincarnate in us* is the true end of personal redemption.

—

The love of God *reincarnate in us* is the true end of personal redemption.

—

"Perfect love" also casts out the tormenting fear of meeting God at the Judgment (see 1 John 4:17-18). "When love comes, fear goes," Barclay writes. "Fear is the characteristic emotion of someone who expects to be punished."[9] In the same vein, Wesley says, "No slavish *fear* can be where *love* reigns; because such *fear hath torment*—and so is inconsistent with the happiness of love." Accordingly, for Wesley there are four classes of Christians. He notes, "A natural man has neither fear nor love; one that is awakened, fear without love; a babe in Christ, love and fear; a father in Christ, love without fear."[10]

Wesley saw this perfect love demonstrated among his early Methodists. "Our people die well," he said. He himself reflected "the art of dying" tradition at its best. On his deathbed the feeble Wesley gathered all his strength and began singing from an Isaac Watts hymn, "I'll praise my Maker while I've breath," causing astonishment to those attending him. Further attempts to sing or speak were unsuccessful. He was able to gather up his strength for one of his last utterances: "The best of all is, God is with us."[11]

Several years ago I was preaching in a fine church in upstate New York. After both the Thursday and Friday night meetings a newly converted lady accosted me at the door with a question: "I know Christ has saved me, but I have this *fear* that troubles me. I don't understand it. Can you tell me what to do about it?"

Preferring to let the Lord answer her question, I simply said, "Just keeping coming to the services." On Saturday evening she was the first to come forward for prayer. After some minutes, God beautifully met her need in sanctifying grace. I was standing at the door Sunday morning after the service greeting the people when she again spoke to me: "Do you remember I spoke to you earlier this week about the fear that was troubling me? Brother Greathouse, *it's gone!"*

Love for God and love for others are indissolubly connected.

Perfect love casts out the tormenting fear of punishment! The only fear that remains is the fear of grieving His love for us. When *God's* love reaches perfection, *our* love is made perfect—and the fear of punishment is cast out. Furthermore, as this passage makes clear, love for God and love for others are indissolubly connected. To quote William Barclay, "As C. H. Dodd puts it, 'The energy of love discharges itself along lines which form a triangle, whose points are God, self, and neighbour.' If God loves us, we are bound to love each other, because it is our destiny to reproduce the life of God in humanity and the life of eternity in time."[12]

"We love [God and others] because he first loved us," John writes (1 John 4:19). The only way to prove that God is within our hearts is for our lives to constantly demonstrate love for others. Therein love reaches perfection. To "be filled with the Spirit" (Eph. 5:18) is to be filled with *love*. Elwood H. Stokes wrote, "Blest, divine, eternal Spirit, / Fill with love, and fill me now."

> *Love divine, all loves excelling,*
> *Joy of heav'n, to earth come down!*
> *Fix in us Thy humble dwelling;*
> *All Thy faithful mercies crown.*
> *Jesus, Thou art all compassion;*
> *Pure, unbounded love Thou art.*
> *Visit us with Thy salvation;*
> *Enter ev'ry trembling heart.*
>
> . . . .
>
> *Come, Almighty to Deliver;*
> *Let us all Thy life receive.*
> *Suddenly return, and never,*
> *Nevermore Thy temples leave.*
> *Thee we would be always blessing,*
> *Serve Thee as Thy hosts above,*
> *Pray and praise Thee without ceasing,*
> *Glory in Thy perfect love.*
>
> —Charles Wesley

Light for Your Spiritual Journey

Cornerstones

Leaf through this chapter again, and mark certain sentences and paragraphs, using these symbols:

△ Put a triangle by the passages that contain an idea of fact that is new to you.

+ Put a plus sign by passages that give you inspi-ration, renewal, comfort, or hope.

⬤ Put a circle by ideas that make you feel uncom-fortable, nervous, or condemned.

⬆ Put an upward arrow by passages that you heartily agree with.

⬇ Mark statements with which you disagree by a downward arrow.

? Put a question mark by passages or statements you don't understand. Talk to a prayer partner or the pastor about them.

Spiritual Stepping-stones

1. Bible Study: Read the entire Epistle of 1 John. Notice and list all the passages that mention *love.*

Note also what 1 John says about *light* and *darkness.*

2. Consider the statement in this chapter that says, "*Erōs* is *need* love; *agapē* is *gift* love." What difference can this awareness make in your personal, family, or professional life?

3. Recall how God and people have blessed you with *gift* love. How precious love is! It is something we cannot be whole without. Novelist John Updike cap-tures the picture of modern culture when an unloved man plots his own suicide while sitting on a crate of self-help books.

Can you think of anyone who could use some *gift* love from you?

Tools to Work With

1. The author of this chapter declares that love to God and love to people are "indissolubly connected." In the previous exercise you were asked about anyone who could use some *gift* love from you. Now record the name, date, and place—in other words, make definite

plans. Tell a friend about your plan (you don't have to give names or many details) so that he or she can serve as your "accountability agent."

2. Memorize this verse from James Russell Lowell:

> *True freedom is to share*
> *All the chains our neighbors wear,*
> *And, with heart and hand, to be*
> *Earnest to make others free.*[13]

3. The gift love from God *(agapē)* can be best shared by those persons in whom the love of God has been perfected. Think about it.

Sanctify them in the truth. . . . And for their
sake I consecrate myself, that they also may
be consecrated in truth. . . . that the love
with which thou hast loved me may be
in them, and I in them.
—John 17:17, 19, 26, RSV

10

True Sanctification

ENTERING INTO THIS SANCTIFYING RELATIONSHIP
with Christ did not come easy for me. Like many, I sought
the *experience* of entire sanctification repeatedly. A year after my conversion, I drove across the continent with my
pastor to attend a camp meeting on the campus of Pasade-
na College in California, where several thousand gathered
daily to hear the inspired preaching of B. F. Neely and
H. V. Miller. One night I went forward to be entirely sanctified; C. W. Ruth, who at one time had been Phineas F. Bresee's associate at Los Angeles First Church of the Nazarene, stepped off the platform and came down to pray with
me. Although I was an earnest and sincere seeker and had
the benefit of Dr. Ruth's prayer and counsel, the blessing
eluded me.

As time passed, my search became desperate. One
May day in the following year I locked myself in my bed-

room after Sunday dinner with the determination to remain there until my need was met. Apparently recognizing for the first time my willingness *to be* sanctified, the Lord exposed to me a sinful pride lurking in my subliminal self. Going to the heart of my problem, a Voice asked, "Would you be willing to return to Arkansas (I was born in Van Buren, Arkansas), spend your ministry there, and the world never know that Billy Greathouse had ever lived?" (I had already answered a call to preach.)

"Yes, Lord," I replied, "I am willing never to be heard of if only You will sanctify my heart."

The Voice then probed more deeply: "Would you be willing to go to China as a missionary?" (This was before the Communist revolution there.)

"Yes, Lord," I responded, "if You will let Ruth go with me." (I already had serious intentions!)

No divine response. Then, probing the depths of my heart, the Voice asked, "Would you be willing to go *alone?*"

After some time of hesitation I answered, "Yes, Lord, if that is Your will."

Instantly I jumped to my feet in ecstasy, my heart flooded with the Spirit and joy unspeakable. (I did not know that my church then would not commission a single male missionary.) My quest was satisfied. *Christ had me— totally!* That Sunday afternoon I prayed with John Wesley,

> *Is there a thing beneath the sun*
> *That strives with Thee my heart to share?*
> *Ah, tear it thence, and reign alone,*
> *The Lord of every motion there!*

In subsequent years the guylines of my life have been severely strained, more than once. But Christ has kept me hedged in at the very point where He met my deepest need, at the point of abandonment to His will. At times my grip on Him has seemed tenuous, but His hold upon me has never weakened, "to the praise of the glory of his grace" (Eph. 1:6, KJV). And I say with John Newton,

> *Through many dangers, toils, and snares*
>   *I have already come.*
> *'Tis grace hath brought me safe thus far,*
>   *And grace will lead me home.*

To be entirely sanctified is more than an experience; it is indeed an experiential reality, but at heart it means to enter into a covenant relationship with Christ, through a willing and purposeful *decision* to permit Him to become *absolute Lord* of our existence. This yielding is the presentation to God that Paul urges in Romans: "Present yourselves to God as those who have been brought from death to life, and present your members to God as instruments of righteousness . . . *for sanctification*" (6:13, 19, emphasis added).

<hr/>

We must come to the crisis of self-abandonment.

<hr/>

To be truly sanctified demands moral decision. We must come to the crisis of self-abandonment to the will of God, a crisis that comes only after we have become painfully aware of our remaining self-centeredness and double-mindedness. Consecration moves on a deeper level than the initial surrender to Christ for pardon. Its motivation is a deepened conviction of the pervasive nature of self-will. It is the frank and contrite acknowledgment of one's pettiness, ambition, pride, and selfishness, and a conscious, willing commitment of the self in love to God. E. Stanley Jones has said,

> There is no love between persons unless there is mutual self-surrender. If either withholds the inmost self, love is blocked. So here.
>
> Then pay the price of a complete surrender. I mean surrender and not dedication. In dedication you still have your hands on the gift—in surrender you let go.

The gift doesn't belong to you any more—it totally and wholly belongs to Another. You now lead a Spirit-led life, instead of a self-led life. You substitute One Will for two wills. You say to yourself, "Let go, let God." You put yourself at the disposal of the Divine. You surrender for better or for worse, for riches or for poverty, in sickness and in health, in life and in death—you will keep yourself only unto Him. *He has you.*[1]

This surrender is both implicit and explicit. It includes the surrender of the total self and of every idol of the heart, however small. The sainted Fénelon wrote, "'That's nothing,' we say. Yes, it is nothing, but a nothing which is all for you; a nothing, which you care enough for to refuse it to God; a nothing which you scorn in words so that you may have an excuse to refuse it, but, at bottom, it is a nothing which you are keeping back from God, and which will be your undoing."[2]

The consecration that opens the way for sanctifying grace has, therefore, been called death to self.[3]

Putting ourselves completely at God's disposal opens the way for Him to complete our inward sanctification by sending the Holy Spirit to purify our hearts and perfect them in love (cf. Rom. 8:3-4 with 13:8-10). In this deeper working of divine grace, the Father answers Jesus' ultimate prayer for us: "that they also may be consecrated in truth . . . that the love with which thou hast loved me may be in them, and I in them" (John 17:19, 26, RSV). *Just as there is a __human__ consecration that precedes and opens the way for true sanctification, there is also a __divine__ consecration that seals and demonstrates it.* Oswald Chambers puts this final point in these words:

> Once you have a personal relationship with Jesus Christ, you will never be moved again. This is the meaning of sanctification. God disapproves of our human efforts to cling to the concept that sanctification is merely an experience, forgetting that even *our sanctification must*

also be sanctified (see John 17:19, emphasis added). I must deliberately give my sanctified life to God for His service, so that He can use me as His hands and His feet.[4]

**I must deliberately give my sanctified life
to God . . . so that He can use me
as His hands and His feet.**

Let us now turn to our Lord's high-priestly prayer for us. Properly understood, this prayer sets forth the cardinal elements of scriptural sanctification.

"Sanctify Them"

First, Jesus prays, "Sanctify them," literally *"Separate them."* The Greek verb *hagiadzō* (sanctify), Adam Clarke explains, is derived from two roots: *ha* (negative) and *gē* (the earth). It signifies, says Clarke, "1. to *consecrate*, to *separate* from the *earth* and *common use*, and to *devote* or *dedicate* to God and his service" and "2. *to make holy or pure.*"[5]

"Sanctify them" thus literally means *"De-earth them!"* That is, "Separate them from the earthy and the sinful to the heavenly and the holy." This process of separation is a metaphor for sanctification found throughout Scripture. Often the Bible compares it to the purification of precious metals. One reference in Malachi is definitive:

> *"Behold, I send My messenger,*
> *And he will prepare the way before Me.*
> *And the Lord, whom you seek,*
> *Will suddenly come to His temple,*
> *Even the Messenger of the covenant,*
> *In whom you delight.*
> *Behold, He is coming,"*
> *Says the LORD of hosts.*

"But who can endure the day of His coming?
And who can stand when He appears?
For He is like a refiner's fire. . . .
He will sit as a refiner and a purifier of silver;
He will purify the sons of Levi,
And purge them as gold and silver,
That they may offer to the LORD
An offering in righteousness."

—3:1-3, NKJV

John the Baptist knew himself to be the appointed forerunner of the promised Refiner. Standing on the banks of the Jordan, he announced: "I baptize you with water for repentance, but he who is coming after me is mightier than I, whose sandals I am not worthy to carry; he will baptize you with the Holy Spirit and with fire" (Matt. 3:11, RSV). The picture here is of the ancient refiner who watched the silver in the crucible and kept the flame burning until the base metal had all come to the top and been skimmed off, until all agitation had ceased, and until he could see his face reflected in the molten silver as in a mirror. That, says George Buttrick, is the parable of Christ's refining baptism with the Holy Spirit.[6] You will observe here a twofold process: first, the silver is mined from the earth, then placed in the crucible to be refined. So our sanctification is twofold: first, we are separated from the world as we respond obediently to the gospel; then we place ourselves in the crucible to be refined, praying all the while,

Let the beauty of Jesus be seen in me—
All His wonderful passion and purity!
O Thou Spirit divine,
All my nature refine
Till the beauty of Jesus be seen in me.

—Albert Orsborn

The apostles had responded obediently to our Lord's call to leave all and follow Him, so that of them He could say, "They are not of the world, even as I am not of the world" (John 17:16, RSV). Nevertheless, although separated from the world to Christ, they still reflected the spirit of the world in their foolish pride, jealousy, anger, and selfish ambition (see Mark 10:32-45). Outwardly sanctified, they were inwardly carnal and worldly-minded. It is one thing to be taken out of the world, but quite another to have the world taken out of us!

The evidence is overwhelming that Jesus' prayer was literally answered for the apostles and for the company of believers gathered with them in the Upper Room on the Day of Pentecost. On that day the glorified Christ baptized them with the promised Spirit (see Acts 2:33), purifying their hearts by faith (15:8-9), perfecting them in love (see 2:37-42), and empowering them as His Spirit-filled Body to continue the ministry He had begun among them as Jesus of Nazareth (see 1:1, 8).

As our Lord continues to pray, He says, however, "I do not pray for these only, but also for those who believe in me through their word" (John 17:20, RSV). This prayer is therefore for *the Church*—for you and me who have believed in Christ through the word of the apostles recorded in the Bible and proclaimed to us by His ministers and teachers.

As believers, we must place ourselves in the crucible of Christ and remain there until the corruption of our sinful hearts comes to our consciousness and we confess it so that the Refiner may remove it (see 1 John 1:7, 9), until all agitation arising from our sinful self-will ceases and subsides in His perfect peace (see Heb. 4:9-10), until our hearts are so transformed that they mirror the very image of Jesus (see 2 Cor. 3:18).

"Consecrate Them"

After praying, "Sanctify them," our Lord continues, "As thou didst send me into the world, so I have sent them into the world. And for their sake I consecrate myself, that they also may be consecrated in truth" (John 17:18-19, RSV).

The Father consecrated the Son and sent Him into the world; so now the Son sanctifies/consecrates the Church and sends them into the world. "The Church exists by mission," Emil Brunner once said, "as fire exists by burning." When fire ceases to burn, it ceases to *be*. So when the Church does not burn with a passion to make Christ known to the world, it ceases to be the Church—and becomes either a sect of the Pharisees or a social club! The Church is the only institution on earth, William Temple reminds us, that exists primarily for nonmembers! It exists chiefly, Jesus reminds us, "so that the world may know that thou hast sent me and hast loved them even as thou hast loved me" (John 17:23, RSV). Therefore, in concluding His high-priestly intercession for the Church, Jesus prays, "O righteous Father . . . I made known to them thy name, and I will make it known, *that the love with which thou hast loved me may be in them, and I in them*" (vv. 25-26, RSV, emphasis added).

Earlier that same evening, referring to His soon departure from them, Jesus assured the apostles, "I will not leave you desolate; I will come to you." Then, with reference to the imminent coming of the Spirit, He said, "In that day you will know that I am in my Father, and you in me, *and I in you*" (14:18, 20, RSV, emphasis added).

I read somewhere of a good brother who felt that his pastor was not giving proper emphasis to the Second Coming. "Pastor," the man asked, "don't you know that Christ is coming back again?" to which he received the reply, "I didn't know He'd ever been away!"

Both had a point. The Blessed Hope, the Parousia, will be the visible appearance of Him who has been with the Church since Pentecost, the day the risen Christ returned in the Spirit to be with the Church forever—and through the Spirit to continue the ministry He began as Jesus of Nazareth. This idea seems to be the one Luke will convey as he begins the Acts of the Apostles: "In the first book, O Theophilus, I have dealt with all that Jesus *began* to do and teach, until the day when he was taken up" (1:1-2, RSV, emphasis added). He would have us understand that Jesus' earthly life and ministry recorded in his Gospel were but the *beginning* of our Lord's personal activity. The ministry He began in the days of His flesh He is now *continuing* through His new Body, the Spirit-filled Church.

The Holy Spirit sanctifies and fills the Church, not as a reservoir, but as a channel. True sanctification is not an end in itself; it becomes the means to a yet higher end. Christ sanctifies us in order that we may become vessels "for noble use, consecrated and useful to the master of the house, ready for any good work" (2 Tim. 2:21, RSV). In *My Lady of the Chimney Corner,* Alexander Irvine tells of his Irish peasant mother, Anna, who one day went to comfort a sorrowing neighbor. "Now tell Him [God] to lay His hand on your tired head in token that He's with you in your distress," Anna quietly counseled her neighbor.

**The Holy Spirit sanctifies and fills
the Church,
not as a reservoir,
but as a channel.**

The prayer was answered. The neighbor said she had received God's comfort, had even felt His hand, "and the hand was just like yours, Anna."

Anna replied, "Yes, the hand was mine, but it was God's too. Sometimes," she said, "God takes a bishop's hand, a doctor's hand, a mother's hand—and sometimes He takes the hand of an old creature like me."[7]

> *Take my life and let it be
> Consecrated, Lord, to Thee.*

Take my hands and let them move
At the impulse of Thy love.
Take my feet and let them be
Swift and beautiful for Thee.

Take my voice and let me sing
Always, only, for my King.
Take my lips and let them be
Filled with messages for Thee.

. . . .

Take my heart—it is Thine own;
It shall be Thy royal throne.

Take my love—my Lord, I pour
At Thy feet its treasure store.
Take myself—and I will be
Ever, only, all for Thee.

—Frances R. Havergal

Light for Your Spiritual Journey

In the place of our usual "Cornerstones," "Spiritual Stepping-stones," and "Tools to Work With," we simply supply a guide for those seeking sanctifying grace.

How to Receive Sanctifying Grace

A. Know That It Is God's Will

"This is the will of God, even your sanctification" (1 Thess. 4:3, KJV). Align your hope and expectation with Paul's prayer for the Thessalonian believers: "May God himself, the God of peace, sanctify you through and through" (1 Thess. 5:23, NIV).

B. Invite God to Prepare Your Heart

God will faithfully lead you to see the depths of in-bred sin—that inward sinfulness that wars against the soul even after acts of sin have been forgiven. He will use the deep hunger of your own soul to lead you. When He has brought you to the place where you love Him with all of your heart, soul, mind, and strength, He bestows sanctifying grace, purifying your heart and filling you with His love. The promise is sure—"If we walk in the light as He is in the light, . . . the blood of Jesus Christ His Son cleanses us from all sin" (1 John 1:7, NKJV).

C. Make Your Consecration Complete

Complete consecration to God is not easy, but it is the only access into the freedom and security that grace offers.

You may wish to make this prayer from John Wesley's handwritten prayer journal your own.

A Prayer of Consecration

O Lord Jesus,
I give thee my body,
my soul,
my substance,
my fame,
my friends,
my liberty,
and my life:
dispose of me and of all that is mine,
as it seems best to thee.

I am now not mine, but thine:
therefore claim me as thy right,
keep me as thy charge,
and love me as thy child.
Fight for me when I am assaulted,
heal me when I am wounded,
and revive me when I am destroyed.[8]

D. Expect Sanctifying Grace Instantaneously by Faith

It sounds like a gradual process of growth at first,

and it does require time for God to prepare the believer's heart. (Certainly there is growth both *toward* and *in* holiness.) But the testimony of God's people throughout the centuries almost always declares that entire sanctification comes instantaneously, after the believer has made consecration complete and in faith opened the very depths of his or her heart to the purging fire of the Spirit.

E. Patiently Following the Hunger of Your Soul

If you follow the deepest hunger of your soul, God will lead you into sanctifying grace and a rich fellowship with Him. Seek with your whole heart, without fretting or tormenting yourself. Resist efforts of zealous persons to get you to claim the blessing prematurely.

Meanwhile, do not put your Christian life on hold. John Wesley taught that the way to "wait" for entire sanctification was to throw yourself into "acts of piety" (prayer, worship, hearing sermons, Communion) and "acts of mercy" (feeding the hungry, instructing the weak, clothing the naked, visiting the sick).

You can trust God to give you His sanctifying grace—the grace Christ provided through the Cross. He died to make it possible. He prayed for your sanctification. It is His will for you. He calls to holiness, and the faithful One will deliver what He promises. Wait patiently before Him.

F. A Prayer for Entire Sanctification

If you are already a Christian, and if you feel led by the Spirit to do so, make this prayer for sanctifying grace your own and dare to believe that God will hear and answer:

O God, I open my heart to its depths before You. Cleanse by the fire of Your Spirit anything that is unlike Christ. Purge my attitudes, my spirit, my affections. Consume all my sinfulness.

Fill me with Your love until I love even those who

persecute or mistreat me. Make me a flame of divine love.

Take all that is mine—I hold nothing back. I claim no right to my wealth, position, or reputation. I give You my body, my soul, my freedom, my friends, and my life. Do with me as You wish. I wish only to know You better and to serve You throughout eternity. In the name of Jesus my Savior, I pray. Amen.[9]

You are of God, little children, and have
overcome them, because He who is in you is
greater than he who is in the world.
—1 John 4:4, NKJV

11

The Secret of
Holy Living

I'LL NEVER MAKE IT!" SHE MOANED. "THE HARDER I
try to live for God, the more miserably I fail. I read my
Bible and pray. I go to church faithfully. I tithe. I try to witness to my neighbors. But every day I fail God. I'll never
make it!"

When her pastor smiled, she broke into tears. "Please
don't make fun of me," she protested; "this is no joke."

"I know it's no joke," he said, "but I thank God you
found it out. You can't make it—but Christ has already
made it for you."

Christ has already won the victory over sin and all the
hosts of darkness arrayed against us. As the apostle John
assures, "You are of God, little children, and have overcome them, because He who is in you is greater than he
who is in the world" (1 John 4:4, NKJV).

Paul puts it this way: "Christ Jesus . . . has become for
us . . . righteousness, holiness and redemption" (1 Cor.

1:30, NIV). Christ is our Holiness as well as our Righteousness. Dying for us, He is our Righteousness; living and reigning in us, He is our Holiness.

Foundational to holy living are the following three truths.

A Distinction to Be Grasped

We must, as we have seen, keep in the forefront of our thinking the distinction between the Law and the gospel. Otherwise, we consign ourselves to confusion and unnecessary condemnation.

We say with Martin Luther that the Law is what God *requires* of us; the gospel is what, on the basis of His promises, He *gives* us.

The old covenant was indeed a covenant of grace, but its central element was Law. Asked which was the great commandment of the Law, Jesus answered: "'You shall love the Lord your God with all your heart. . . . You shall love your neighbor as yourself.' On these two commandments hang all the law and the prophets" (Matt. 22:37, 39-40).

The weakness of the old covenant was that it contained no offer of the life-giving, sanctifying Spirit. The distinctive nature of the new covenant is precisely the promise of the Spirit. Through His Son, "God has done what the law, weakened by the flesh, could not do" (Rom. 8:3). Through Christ, God has vanquished sin and opened the floodgates of the sanctifying Spirit (see vv. 1-4).

The Law remains the divine requirement, deepened and refined by Jesus; but the good news is that the Spirit who fulfills the Law has been given! If the central feature of the old covenant is Law (what God commands), the heart of the new is the gospel (what God gives according to His promise).

A Promise to Be Appropriated

Writing to the Galatians, who were being seduced by Jewish legalists to return to the law, Paul penned, "You foolish Galatians! Who has bewitched you? Before your very eyes Jesus Christ was clearly portrayed as crucified. I would like to learn just one thing from you: Did you receive the Spirit by observing the law, or by believing what you heard? Are you so foolish? After beginning with the Spirit, are you now trying to attain your goal [literally, "being perfected," NASB] by human effort?" (3:1-3, NIV).

To turn back from *Christ-reliance* to *self-effort* is the same as to "rely on works of the law" (v. 10, RSV). And this means to revert to the bondage of fear (see Rom. 8:15, KJV).

Unfortunately, those who take seriously God's call to holiness often fall into the trap of slavish fear. John Wesley saw clearly that pardoning love is at the root of it all. The root of holiness is the assurance that in Christ Jesus "there is now no condemnation" (Rom. 8:1, NIV). Thank God, we are "accepted in the beloved" (Eph. 1:6, KJV). *But we must "accept our acceptance"!* In his sermon on "Satan's Devices," Wesley warns that one of Satan's most potent weapons is to cause us to doubt our acceptance by God because of our shortcomings. To give way to doubt is to forfeit first our joy, then our peace, and finally our faith and love.

We must rest in the promises of God. "There is therefore now no condemnation" if we "walk not after the flesh, but after the Spirit" (Rom. 8:1, KJV). To come to the point where we can exercise faith for the deeper blessing of heart holiness, we must maintain a joyous sense of our acceptance. We enter the experience of entire sanctification by faith alone. We begin in the Spirit, and we are perfected in the Spirit. Salvation is "by faith from first to last, just as it is written: 'The righteous will live by faith'" (Rom. 1:17, NIV).

What is the faith by which we are truly sanctified and perfected in God's love? Focus again on the salient points of John Wesley's answer based on Heb. 11:1 and Rom. 10:17:

> It is a divine evidence and conviction, First, that God hath promised it in the Holy Scripture. . . .

It is a divine evidence and conviction, Secondly, that what God hath promised He is able to perform. . . .

It is, Thirdly, a divine evidence and conviction that He is able and willing to do it now. . . .

To this confidence, that God is both able and willing to sanctify us now, there needs to be added one thing more,—a divine evidence and conviction that He doeth it. In that hour it is done: God says to the inmost soul, "According to thy faith be it unto thee!"[1]

"May God himself, the God of peace, sanctify you through and through. May your whole spirit, soul and body be kept blameless at the coming of our Lord Jesus Christ. The one who calls you is faithful and he will do it" (1 Thess. 5:23-24, NIV).

A Grace to Be Lived

Remember, "Christ Jesus . . . has become for us . . . holiness" (1 Cor. 1:30, NIV). To be truly sanctified is to be able to say with Paul, "My present life is not that of the old 'I,' but the living Christ within" (Gal. 2:20, PHILLIPS). It is to have experienced the answer to Paul's prayer in Ephesians: "That out of his glorious riches he may strengthen you with power through his Spirit in your inner being, so that Christ may dwell in your hearts through faith. . . . that you may be filled to the measure of all the fullness of God" (3:16-17, 19, NIV).

To be Christian, said theologian Dietrich Bonhoeffer, is "to have the precise space once occupied by the old man now to be occupied by Jesus Christ."

This is to be holy; for to be truly Christian is one and the same thing as to be holy.

Christ living and reigning in me through the power of the indwelling Spirit is the essence of holiness. The victory that overcomes the world is the faith that "greater is he that is in you, than he that is in the world" (1 John 4:4, KJV).

"If we live by the Spirit," Paul urges, "let us also walk

by the Spirit" (Gal. 5:25, RSV). Walking by the Spirit is remembering that apart from Christ we "can do nothing" (John 15:5). It is maintaining a moment-by-moment dependence upon Him as our Life.

◄━◄

At the deepest, holiness is not a matter of holy habit patterns; these are simply a cut-flower arrangement if we do not sustain an intimate relationship with Christ.

◄━◄

At the deepest, holiness is not a matter of holy habit patterns; these are simply a cut-flower arrangement if we do not sustain an intimate relationship with Christ. But if we abide in Him, His life becomes our life, His love our love, and His joy our joy.

The secret of holy living is to permit *Christ* to live His life of holy love *in us!*

◄━◄

Light for Your Spiritual Journey

Cornerstones

1. **Can you live the holy life in your own strength?**

About 1 billion people on our planet practice the religions of Buddhism or Hinduism. In spite of some good points, these are religions of despair. There is little hope of getting off the wheel of repeated reincarnations. You have to keep on living one life after another until you get it right. The law, the measurements are there. Buddhists, for example, start with Four Noble Truths, add the Eightfold Path of Right Living, tack on Ten Commandments, and add 250 rules for men and 500 rules for women. (Females have more rules because they are inferior. In fact, classic Buddhism teaches that before a woman can scale the ladder of enlightenment and disappear into Nirvana, she must be reborn as a male.) Hindus have equally stringent laws and regulations. In their teachings there is no Savior, no redeeming grace. Each person must do it himself. And the most lofty goal is to fade into the nonpersonal existence of Nirvana, where all individuality is lost forever. The end of personal existence is seen as the most hopeful end to the cycles of reincarnations, at which there is little help for enlightenment or hope for salvation. Live poorly, and you might come back as a beggar, a donkey, a cow, or an insect. This old folk song from India catches the despair:

> How many births are past, I cannot tell.
> How many yet to come no man can say:
> But this alone I know, and know full well,
> That pain and grief embitter all the way.[2]

In *Misguiding Lights?* Mark Albrecht tells of his encounter with a loincloth-garbed man in north India. He was painted with Hindu symbols, including three white stripes signifying his devotion to Shiva the Destroyer. On a cold day he sat in the opening of a small cave, shivering behind his matted hair and beard.

"Why are you doing this?" Mark asked.

He smiled only slightly as he replied in excellent English: "You may not understand. I was born to a wealthy family in Bombay and have a university degree. At the age of 30 I realized it was all meaningless."

He went on to say that *samsara* was escorting him through his 1,742nd lifetime. He had had enough. He said that to keep his comfortable life in Bombay would mean even more lifetimes on the agonizing wheel of existence. So he decided to earn his salvation (his enlightenment) by renouncing it all and living as an ascetic holy man.

"This means I meditate eight hours each day and

eat only roots, berries, wild grains, and plants. I drink from the holy River Ganges. . . . When I die, I shall not . . . return to this planet of suffering and woe. I have attained enlightenment."[3]

Compare this with this statement from chapter 11: "You can't make it—but Christ has already made it for you." In Christianity, hope is knee deep.

2. Foundation Principles

Review the cornerstones that appear in the outline of this chapter. Study the content of each section, and reduce it to one timeless principle stated in your own words.

A Distinction to Be Grasped
Timeless Principle: _____

_____

_____

A Promise to Be Appropriated
Timeless Principle: _____

_____

_____

A Grace to Be Lived
Timeless Principle: _____

_____

_____

Spiritual Stepping-stones

A Seven-Point Quiz

1. One time that I failed to distinguish between Law and grace (or gospel) was when I _____

_____

2. How long has it been since Satan cited your shortcomings and led you to doubt your acceptance by God? How was your confidence restored? Was it restored?

Read again the reference to John Wesley's sermon "Satan's Devices" in this chapter.

3. Martin Luther saw that the Law is what God *requires* of us, but the gospel (grace) is what He *gives* us. How does this insight affect your spiritual life right now?

4. One time when I turned from *Christ-reliance* to *self-reliance* was _____

_____

_____.

5. Contemplate Rom. 8:3: "God has done what the law, weakened by the flesh, could not do." If you were to speak about this verse in family devotions tonight, what would you say?

6. In this chapter we are urged to walk in the Spirit, "maintaining a moment-by-moment dependence on Christ's Spirit. How skillful have you been at this? What is one thing you could do to improve your record at living in the Spirit moment by moment?

7. Near the end of the chapter the author uses a metaphor of a "cut-flower arrangement." What does this mean to you?

Tools to Work With

1. Who said?

One of the crucial elements in making a case or persuading an audience is the quality of the evidence presented. That is, who testified for you? Did you quote John the apostle or Johnny Cochran, Martin Luther or Martin Mull?

In this chapter the author quoted three Bible writers. Look to see what they had to say about holiness:

Paul

Matthew

John

The author also recruited these people to testify for his case:

John Wesley

Lelia N. Morris

Dietrich Bonhoeffer

Martin Luther

Jack Ford

Look over what these "witnesses" had to say. Ponder their insights. Enter into your spiritual life journal the words from the author(s) that mean the most to you right now.

2. Living the Secret

The last sentence of the chapter reveals the secret of holy living—*letting Christ live His holy life through you.*

Write the secret on a card. State it in the form of a pledge to let Christ live His holy life through you. Put the card in your Bible, your purse or wallet, on your refrigerator door—wherever it will be constantly before you.

We rejoice in the hope of the glory of God . . .
because God has poured out his love
into our hearts by the Holy Spirit,
whom he has given us.
—Rom. 5:2, 5, NIV

12

Love Made Perfect, Foretaste of Glory

As WE HAVE NOTED THROUGHOUT THESE PAGES, the distinctive feature of the Christian dispensation—that which distinguishes the gospel from the Law—is the gift of the Holy Spirit, bringing to fulfillment all the promises of the Old Testament to His people and, as we shall now see, ushering in the "last days" of salvation history.

This fulfilled promise of God was the dramatic announcement of the apostle Peter on the Day of Pentecost:

This is what was spoken by the prophet Joel:
"And it shall come to pass in the last days,
  says God,
That I will pour out of My Spirit on all flesh;
Your sons and your daughters shall prophesy,
Your young men shall see visions,
Your old men shall dream dreams.

> *And on My menservants and on My*
> *maidservants*
> *I will pour out My Spirit in those days;*
> *And they shall prophesy.*
> *I will show wonders in heaven above*
> *And signs in the earth beneath:*
> *Blood and fire and vapor of smoke.*
> *The sun shall be turned into darkness,*
> *And the moon into blood,*
> *Before the coming of the great and notable day of*
> *the LORD.*
> *And it shall come to pass that whoever calls on*
> *the name of the LORD shall be saved"*
>
> (Acts 2:16-21, NKJV).

The "last days" of which Joel here speaks are the promised age of salvation, the age of the Spirit, which began at Pentecost and will continue until "the great and notable day of the LORD," when Christ shall return in final redemption and judgment.

God's outpoured Spirit is His outpoured love.

In a text that has been spoken of as "the Pentecost of Romans," the apostle Paul gives us the ethical significance of the gift of the Holy Spirit in the age of salvation: "God has poured out his love in our hearts by the Holy Spirit whom he has given us" (Rom. 5:5, NIV). God's outpoured Spirit is His outpoured love.

In order to grasp the full, redemptive significance of Paul's text, we must put it in its context. "Therefore, since we have been justified through faith, we have peace with God through our Lord Jesus Christ, through whom we have gained access by faith into this grace in which we now stand. And we rejoice in the hope of the glory of God. Not only so, but we also rejoice in our sufferings, because we know that suffering produces perseverance; perseverance, character; and character, hope. And hope does not disappoint us, because God has poured out his love into our hearts by the Holy Spirit, whom he has given us" (Rom. 5:1-5, NIV).

God "poured out his love" in the apostles' hearts on the Day of Pentecost, impelling them to pour out their lives in love for Him and service to their fellow creatures, in the confident expectation that God, who inaugurated His kingdom by raising His Son from the dead—exalting the crucified Jesus to His own right hand—would consummate that Kingdom by sending His Son a second time finally to redeem His people and judge the world.

In the same manner, when the Father pours His love out in our hearts by the Holy Spirit, we also are inflamed with a holy passion to know and love God and to pour out our lives for others, being confident of this, that he who has begun this good work in us "will bring it to completion by the day of Jesus Christ" (Phil. 1:6). Such is the faith, the love, and the hope of the gospel.

God's love shed abroad in our hearts by the Holy Spirit is at once our **holiness** and our **hope.**

Let us look briefly at each of these truths.

First, God's love flooding our hearts is our holiness —the fulfillment of the love command of His Law.

The Great Commandment of the Law

Let us review a point we have noted previously. When asked by the scribe which was the greatest commandment of the Law, Jesus replied, *"'You shall love the Lord your God with all your heart, with all your soul, and with all your mind.'* This is the first and great commandment. And the second is like it: *'You shall love your neighbor as yourself.'* On these two commandments hang all the Law and the Prophets" (Matt. 22:36-40, NKJV).

Law and Gospel

Martin Luther insisted that if you know the difference between the Law and the gospel, you are a theologian. Consider, therefore, that while the Law of God commands perfect love (Deut. 6:4-5; Lev. 19:18), it cannot give this love. But listen to the gospel of God: "God has done what the law, weakened by the flesh, could not do: by sending his own Son in the likeness of sinful flesh, and to deal with sin, he condemned sin in the flesh, so that the just requirement of the law [love for God and others—5:5; 13:8-10] might be fulfilled in us, who walk not according to the flesh but according to the Spirit" (Rom. 8:3-4). God who pours out His love in our hearts by the Holy Spirit by that action creates within us the obedience commanded by the Law.

Love Made Perfect

Listen to the apostle John as he writes in his First Epistle, "Beloved, let us love one another, because love is from God; everyone who loves is born of God and knows God. Whoever does not love does not know God, for God is love. . . . If we love one another [and "obey his word," 2:5], God lives in us, and his love is perfected in us. . . . God is love, and those who abide in love abide in God, and God abides in them. Love has been perfected among us in this: that we may have boldness on the day of judgment, because as he is, so are we in this world" (4:7-8, 12, 16-17).

While the primary reference to the pronoun "he" in verse 17 above is probably to Christ (see p. 107), Augustine finds here a parallel to Jesus' ethic in the Sermon on the Mount. As God the Father loves all persons unconditionally—His enemies as well as His friends—so do "we in this world," if we love with His unconditional *agapē*. To love in this manner is to "be perfect, just as our heavenly Father is perfect" (see Matt. 5:48).[1] "We know it to be *of* but not *from* us," says Bonnie Thurston, "when, in our desire to follow after Jesus, we can 'do good to' when we do not 'feel good toward.'"[2]

Paul's prayer for the Ephesians is that they may be thus perfected in love: "I bow my knees before the Father. . . . I pray that, according to the riches of his glory, . . . you may be strengthened in your inner being with power through his Spirit, . . . that Christ may dwell in your hearts through faith, as you are being rooted and grounded in love. . . . that you may be filled with all the fullness of God" (3:14, 16-17, 19).

God's love poured out in our hearts and perfected in us by the infilling of the Spirit is the crowning promise of the Christian dispensation. "You can go no higher than this," says Wesley, "till you are carried into Abraham's bosom."[3]

Second, and fully as important, God's love poured out in our hearts by the Holy Spirit is also our *hope*—the guarantee and first installment of the glory that will be ours when Christ returns.

"The kingdom of God is not food and drink, but righteousness and peace and joy in the Holy Spirit" (Rom. 14:17, NKJV). To experience these blessings in the Spirit, says Wesley, is to have "heaven already opened in the soul." The Holy Spirit "inspires the Christian soul with that even, solid joy, which arises from the testimony of the Spirit that he is a child of God; and that gives him to 'rejoice with joy unspeakable, in hope of the glory of God. . . .'"[4]

The Seal and Earnest of the Spirit

"For in him every one of God's promises is a 'Yes,'" Paul writes in 2 Cor. 1:20-22. "For this reason it is through him that we say the 'Amen,' to the glory of God. . . . It is God who establishes us with you in Christ and has anointed us, by putting his seal on us and giving us his Spirit in our hearts as a first installment." Again in Eph. 1:13-14 he says. "In him . . . when you had . . . believed in him, [you] were marked with the seal of the promised Holy Spirit; . . . the pledge ("earnest," KJV) of our inheritance toward redemption as God's own people, to the praise of his glory."

In these texts we find a thrilling and precious metaphor. Letters of all kinds and official documents were in those days sealed with wax. A warm blob of wax was placed on the letter or document; the sender or signer then pressed his signet into the wax, making an official seal. *The Holy Spirit in the believer's life is the divine Seal of approval upon that life.* "God's solid foundation stands firm, sealed with this inscription: 'The Lord knows those who are his,' and, 'Everyone who confesses the name of the Lord must turn away from wickedness'" (2 Tim. 2:19, NIV). If the submissive heart is the warm and plastic wax, the Holy Spirit is the Seal—and the image of Christ is the visible mark of identification. The Seal is at once an assurance to the believer and a sign to the world.

The metaphor of the earnest suggests another beautiful truth. The earnest is a partial payment that binds the agreement and obliges both the buyer and seller to complete the transaction. The gift of the Holy Spirit is the first installment, as it were, of the infinite treasure God plans to bestow upon us when Christ returns to complete our salvation. So long as we abide in God, and He abides in us, we have the *guarantee,* as well as the *foretaste,* of heaven. "And do not grieve the Holy Spirit of God," Paul admonishes, "by whom you were sealed for the day of redemption" (Eph. 4:30, NKJV). So long as we abide in God's love, and His love abides in us, and we "turn away from wickedness," the Spirit's seal is ours, and we have the assurance, and the foretaste, of heaven.

"The Firstfruits of the Spirit"

In Rom. 8 Paul uses another metaphor, speaking of *"the firstfruits of the Spirit"* that Christians enjoy (v. 23, KJV).

Ponder this imagery. Just as the grapes, the milk, and the honey that Caleb and Joshua brought out of Canaan were a foretaste of the Promised Land (if they would but go in and possess it), so the Holy Spirit is the *"firstfruits,"* the foretaste of the glory that will be ours when we see Christ.

As C. F. Butler taught us to sing,

> *Once heaven seemed a far-off place,*
> *Till Jesus showed His smiling face.*
> *Now it's begun within my soul;*
> *'Twill last while endless ages roll.*
>
> *Oh, hallelujah, yes, 'tis heaven,*
> *'Tis heaven to know my sins forgiven!*
> *On land or sea, what matters where?*
> *Where Jesus is, 'tis heaven there.*

This foretaste of heaven is that of which Paul is speaking in our passage. "Therefore, having been justified by faith, we have peace with God through our Lord Jesus Christ, through whom also we have access by faith into this grace in which we stand, and rejoice in hope of the glory of God. And not only that, but we also glory in tribulations, knowing that tribulation produces perseverance; and perseverance, character; and character, hope. Now hope does not disappoint, because the love of God has been poured out in our hearts by the Holy Spirit who was given to us" (Rom. 5:1-5, NKJV).

The Holy Spirit Witnesses to Christ's Victory

The Holy Spirit dwelling in us is the experiential counterpart, *the inward witness* to Christ's present heavenly reign and future coming in glory. Think of it. The indwelling Holy Spirit produces within us the certainty that Christ, by His death and resurrection, has crushed the serpent's head in our behalf, securing our salvation. "The ruler of this world is judged" (John 16:11, NKJV). Satan is a defeated foe!

In His cross the incarnate Son of God dethroned Satan, destroyed sin, and abolished death. He is *Christus Victor!* Even though Satan's tail still wriggles and creates chaos (as the early fathers put it), his final doom is sure! "The kingdoms of this world have become the kingdoms of our Lord and of His Christ, and He shall reign forever and ever!" (Rev. 11:15, NKJV.)

<hr />

The Holy Spirit dwelling in our hearts makes *Christ's victory over evil our present victory* over Satan, sin, and death, assuring us of immortality and eternal life!

<hr />

What if an asteroid should someday come crashing into our planet? We have received "a kingdom that cannot be shaken" (Heb. 12:28). "My kingdom is not of this world," says Jesus (John 18:36, KJV). "This hope we have as an anchor of the soul, both sure and steadfast, and which enters the Presence behind the veil, where the forerunner has entered for us, even Jesus" (Heb. 6:19-20, NKJV). "We do not yet see all things put under him," the writer of Hebrews acknowledges. "But we see Jesus, who was made a little lower than the angels, for the suffering of death crowned with glory and honor, that He, by the grace of God, might taste death for everyone" (2:8-9, NKJV).

Christ's Victory Ours in the Holy Spirit

Paul sums up all this when he writes, *"Hope does not disappoint us, because God has poured out his love into our hearts by the Holy Spirit, whom he has given us."* The Holy Spirit dwelling in our hearts makes *Christ's victory over evil our present victory* over Satan, sin, and death, assuring us of immortality and eternal life!

By God's grace and the power of the Holy Spirit we "have overcome" the devil and the forces of evil, "because greater is he that is in you, than he that is in the world" (1 John 4:4, KJV)! And because God in Christ has "condemned sin in the flesh," I can testify, "The law of the Spirit of life in Christ Jesus has set me free from the law of sin and death" (Rom. 8:3, 2, RSV). And when God's love is made perfect in us, "we may have boldness on the day of judgment, because as he is, so are we in this world. There is no fear in love, but perfect love casts out fear" (1 John 4:17-18). "Thanks be to God, who gives us the victory through our Lord Jesus Christ" (1 Cor. 15:57, NKJV)!

"Heaven Already Opened in Our Souls"

In the Holy Spirit, Hebrews tells us, we "have tasted . . . the powers of the age to come" (6:4-5). Charles Wesley has given this glorious truth poetic expression:

> Oh, what a blessed hope is ours!
>   While here on earth we stay,
> We more than taste the heavenly powers,
>   And antedate that day.
>
> We feel the resurrection near,
>   Our life in Christ concealed;
> And with His glorious presence here
>   Our earthen vessels filled.

A small boy was flying a kite that was so high it could not be seen. A man observing the lad holding the string to the invisible kite asked him, "What are you doing?" "Flying my kite." "How do you know the kite is up there? You can't see it." "No," the boy responded, "but I know it's up there, because I can feel its pull." The Holy Spirit flooding our hearts with divine love is the heavenly pull that assures us of our final salvation. "Hope does not disappoint us, because God has poured out his love into our hearts by the Holy Spirit, whom he has given us."

"We speak the wisdom of God in a mystery," Paul writes in 1 Corinthians. "As it is written:

> *'Eye has not seen, nor ear heard,*
> *Nor have entered into the heart of man*
> *The things which God has prepared for those who love*
> *Him.'*

"*But God has revealed them to us through His Spirit*" (2:7, 9-10, NKJV, last line, emphasis added)! *Amen!*

Light for Your Spiritual Journey

Cornerstones

This chapter is constructed around some key building blocks. Review the central function and the scriptural foundation of each of the following keys to this chapter.

Love

Holiness

Service

Hope

Heaven

Stepping-stones

1. Building Bridges

The task of every teacher, speaker, and preacher is to build bridges *from* the principles, theories, and ideas underlying their presentation to the everyday lives of the students or hearers. Sometimes the bridges connect the ancient with the modern or the abstract with the concrete. Sometimes the task is to build a bridge connecting theory and practice or the general and the specific or the negative and the positive. Consider the cornerstones above to be bridge pillars. Build a bridge between one or more of the pillars and your own personal life. The bridge may connect with your life at the point of your:

physical being

family life

social life

vocational life

devotional life

service to God, the church, other people

2. For Meditation

Transformation:

"O Son of God, do a miracle for me, and change my heart; Thy having taken [on] flesh to redeem me was more difficult than to transform my wickedness."

Old Irish prayer, 1448

Christian Service:

"May I be an island in the sea, may I be a hill on the land, may I be a star when the moon wanes, may I be a staff to the weak one."   *Ancient Scottish proverb*

Hope:

"I know the plans I have for you . . . plans to give you hope and a future."   *Jeremiah 29:11, NIV*

Tools to Work With

Pass It On

Now that you have read and worked and prayed your way through this book, it has become a tool you can use to help someone else. Pass it on. Give or loan the book to someone who could profit from the same study that you have completed.

Compose a note or letter to the person to whom you will give or loan this book. Include a word of appreciation for the person. Cite a good character trait, a good example, or some deed of helpfulness to you or others. Also include a few sentences about how this book helped you. Suggest that the two of you get together to talk about the book and the concerns, challenges, and answers that it offers.

Notes

Foreword

1. William M. Greathouse, "Before I Go Let Me Say . . . ," *Herald of Holiness*, July 1989, 6.

2. Ibid., 7.

Chapter 1

1. George Croft Cell, *The Rediscovery of John Wesley* (New York: Henry Holt and Co., 1935), 359.

2. Adam Clarke, *Christian Theology*, ed. Samuel Dunn (New York: T. Mason and G. Lane, 1840), 183.

3. Richard P. Heitzenrater, *Wesley and the People Called Methodists* (Nashville: Abingdon Press, 1995), 121.

4. John Wesley, "The Circumcision of the Heart," in *Wesley's Standard Sermons*, ed. Edward H. Sugden (London: Epworth Press, 1921), 1:267.

5. *The Letters of the Rev. John Wesley*, ed. John Telford (London: Epworth Press, 1931), 5:322.

6. John Wesley, *A Plain Account of Christian Perfection* (Kansas City: Beacon Hill Press of Kansas City, 1966), 83.

7. Ibid., 54.

8. Ibid., 83.

9. *Letters*, 4:208.

10. Wesley, A *Plain Account*, 82.

11. Ibid., 82-83.

12. *John Wesley's Sunday Service of the Methodists in North America* (Nashville: The United Methodist Publishing House and the United Methodist Board of Higher Education and Ministry, 1984), 125.

Chapter 2

1. Norman H. Snaith, *The Distinctive Ideas of the Old Testament* (London: Epworth Press, 1960), 21.

2. Ibid., 43.

3. A term coined by Rudolf Otto, *The Idea of the Holy: An Inquiry into the Non-rational Factor in the Idea of the Divine and Its Relation to the Rational*, trans. John W. Harvey, 2nd ed. (London: Oxford University Press, 1950).

4. Snaith, *Distinctive Ideas*, 30.

5. Ibid.

6. Donald E. Demaray, ed., *The Daily Wesley*, trans. Paul Gerhardt (Anderson, Ind.: Bristol House, 1994), 95.

7. Ibid., 48.

8. George Allen Turner, *The Vision Which Transforms* (Kansas City: Beacon Hill Press, 1964), 17.

9. Ibid.

10. Theodorus C. Vriezen, *An Outline of Old Testament Theology* (Newton, Mass.: Charles T. Bradford Co., 1958).

11. John W. Harvey, preface to Otto, *The Idea of the Holy*, xviii.

Chapter 3

1. Statement of the National Conference of Catholic Bishops, 1975; cited by Walter Harrelson and Randall M. Falk, *Jews and Christians: A Troubled Family* (Nashville: Abingdon Press, 1991), 14.

2. George Allen Turner, *The More Excellent Way* (Winona Lake, Ind.: Light and Life Press, 1952), 31.

3. Colin W. Williams, *John Wesley's Theology Today* (London: Epworth Press, 1960), 179.

4. Albert Outler, *John Wesley* (New York: Oxford University Press, 1964), 157-58.

5. Richard J. Foster, *Freedom of Simplicity* (San Francisco: Harper and Row Publishers, 1981), 36.

6. John Wesley, "On a Single Eye," Sermon 118 in *The Works of John Wesley*, ed. Thomas Jackson, 3rd ed. (reprint, Kansas City: Beacon Hill Press of Kansas City, 1979), 7:297.

7. Søren Kierkegaard, *Purity of Heart Is to Will One Thing* (New York: Harper and Brothers, 1956), 72.

8. Stephen Green, in *Biblical Resources for Holiness Preaching: From Text to Sermon*, ed. H. Ray Dunning and Neil B. Wiseman (Kansas City: Beacon Hill Press of Kansas City, 1990), 105.

9. See Luke 1:6; 1 Cor. 1:8; Eph. 1:4; 5:27 (NASB); Phil. 2:15; Col. 1:22-23; 1 Thess. 5:23; 2 Pet. 3:14 (KJV).

10. *Theological Dictionary of the Bible*, ed. Gerhard Kittel and Gerhard Friedrich (Grand Rapids: William B. Eerdmans Publishing Co., 1972), 8:73-77.

11. William Barclay, *The Letters to the Galatians and Ephesians*, in *The Daily Study Bible* (Philadelphia: Westminster Press, 1977), 78-79.

12. Turner, *The Vision Which Transforms*, 45.

13. Ibid., 46.

14. Attributed to Samuel Goldwyn by Margaret Minor and Hugh Rawson in *New International Dictionary of Quotations* (New York: Signet, a division of Penguin Books, 1994), 172.

Chapter 4

1. Wallace Hamilton, *Who Goes There?* (Westwood, N.J.: Fleming H. Revell Co., 1958), 36-37.

2. Wesley, "The Scripture Way of Salvation," in *Wesley's Standard Sermons*, 2:448, 457.

3. Gerhard Ebeling, *Luther: An Introduction to His Thought* (Philadelphia: Fortress Press, 1972), 110-11.

4. *Works of Martin Luther,* translated with introductions and notes (Philadelphia: Muhlenberg Press, 1932), 6:451.

5. Wesley, "The Circumcision of the Heart," 1:267.

6. *John Wesley's Sunday Service of the Methodists in North America,* 125.

7. Wesley, "The Way to the Kingdom," Sermon 7 in *Works*, 5:79.

8. Wesley, "Upon Our Lord's Sermon on the Mount," Discourse 8, Sermon 28 in *Works*, 5:376-77.

9. Samuel Medley, "The Glorious Hope" in *Worship in Song* (Kansas City: Lillenas Publishing Co., 1972), No. 293.

Chapter 5

1. Irenaeus, *Against the Heresies,* trans. Dominic J. Unger (New York: Paulist Press, 1992), 3.14.7.

2. Ibid.

3. Gustaf Aulén, *Christus Victor,* trans. A. G. Hebert (New York: Macmillan Co., 1951); see esp. pp. 16-35.

4. C. H. Dodd, *The Epistle to the Romans,* in *The Moffatt New Testament Commentary* (New York: Harper and Brothers Publishers, 1932), 93.

5. John Wesley, *Explanatory Notes upon the New Testament* (London: Epworth Press, 1950), 546.

6. Wesley D. Tracy, ed., *The Redeemed Will Walk There: Sermons on the Life of Holiness* (Kansas City: Beacon Hill Press of Kansas City, 1983), 44.

7. Irenaeus, *Against the Heresies* 2.22.4.

Chapter 6

1. Franz J. Leenhardt, *The Epistle to the Romans* (Cleveland and New York: World Publishing Co., 1957), 103-4.

2. This is the force of the Greek aorist tense here in Rom. 6.

3. J. A. T. Robinson, *The Body* (London: SCM Press, 1952), 28.

4. William E. Sangster, *The Pure in Heart* (New York and Nashville: Abingdon Press, 1964), 235-36. This is the thesis of the late Nazarene general superintendent R. T. Williams in his book *Temptation: A Neglected Theme* (Kansas City: Nazarene Publishing House, 1920).

5. Bill Bright, *How to Walk in the Spirit* (San Bernardino, Calif.: Campus Crusade for Christ, 1971), 47-48.

6. From a prayer of Jeremy Taylor, quoted by Bob and Michael W. Benson, *Disciplines of the Inner Life* (Waco, Tex.: Word Books, 1985), 22.

Chapter 7

1. John Wesley, "A Plain Account of Christian Perfection," in *Works,* 11:387.

2. J. S. Whale, *Christian Doctrine* (New York: The MacMillan Co., 1945), 53.

3. Wesley, "On Working Out Our Own Salvation," Sermon 85 in *Works,* 6:509.

4. Ibid.

5. Wesley, "On Patience," Sermon 83 in *Works,* 6:488-89.

6. P. F. Bresee, "Pentecost," in *Sermons from Matthew's Gospel* (Kansas City: Nazarene Publishing House, n.d.), 39.

7. Wesley, "On Patience," 6:489.

8. Ibid.

9. Wesley, "A Plain Account," 11:402.

10. Wesley, "On Working Out Our Own Salvation," 6:509.

11. Karl Barth, *The Epistle to the Romans* (London: Oxford University Press, 1933), 314.

Chapter 8

1. George Lyons, "Modeling the Holiness Ethos: A Study Based on First Thessalonians," *Wesleyan Theological Journal* 30, No. 1 (spring 1995): 188-89.

2. Ibid., 194.

3. Daniel Brett Spross, "Sanctification in the Thessalonian Epistles in a Canonical Context" (Ph.D. diss., Southern Baptist Theological Seminary, 1987), 21 (citing J. B. Lightfoot). The Greek verb *katartisai* and its derivatives occur in the New Testament with a wide variety of meanings. The disciples were "*mending* their nets" (Matt. 4:21; Mark 1:19; emphasis added). The fractious Corinthians were commanded to "*become perfect*" (2 Cor. 13:9, emphasis added). The NRSV rendering of *katartisai,* "*restore*" (emphasis added), violates the context; there is no evidence in the Epistle of any loss of faith on the part of the Thessalonians.

4. Suggested in private conversation by Alex R. G. Deasley.

5. Lyons, "Modeling the Holiness Ethos," 191-92.

6. The adverb translated "worthy" does not imply that moral living is a means of earning God's call to Kingdom glory. Rather, it is "a recognition that God's call to future salvation makes certain behaviors 'appropriate' in the present. A holy God demands a holy people (cf. 1 Pet. 1:13-16)" (Lyons, "Modeling the Holiness Ethos," 203).

7. Spross, "Sanctification in the Thessalonian Epistles," 34.

8. Ibid., 41-42.

9. Ibid., 43.

10. Lyons, "Modeling the Holiness Ethos," 192. The clearest illustration of this necessary human cooperation in order to effect sanctification is Paul's injunction in Rom. 6:12-19.

11. Spross, "Sanctification in the Thessalonian Epistles," 44, quoting Ernest Best, *A Commentary on the First and Second Epistles to the Thessalonians* (New York: Harper and Row, 1972), 242.

12. Spross, "Sanctification," 46, quoting D. E. H. Whiteley, *The Theology of St. Paul* (London: Oxford University Press, 1964), 85.

13. Leon Morris, "The First and Second Epistles to the Thessalonians," in *The New International Commentary on the New Testament* (Grand Rapids: William B. Eerdmans Publishing Co., 1959), 180.

14. Spross, "Sanctification in the Thessalonian Epistles," 46.

15. Morris, "Thessalonians," 80. The second half of the adverb, *teleis,* derives from the root *telos,* meaning "end," "goal," "purpose." D. Edmond Hiebert explains *holoteleis:* "wholly affecting the end, reaching the intended goal, hence has here the force of no part being left untouched" (*A Call to Readiness: The Thessalonian Epistles* [Chicago: Moody Press, 1971], 251).

16. Clarke, *Christian Theology,* 183.

17. Thus, John Wesley uses "entire sanctification" and "Christian perfection" interchangeably.

18. Spross, "Sanctification in the Thessalonian Epistles," 50, quoting Gordon Pitts Wiles, "The Function of Intercessory Prayer in Paul's Apostolic Ministry with Special Reference to the First Epistle to the Thessalonians" (Ph.D. diss., Yale University, 1965), 132.

19. Spross, "Sanctification," 51, quoting Best, *Thessalonians,* 182.

20. Wesley, "The Scripture Way of Salvation," 2:457-59.

21. Wesley, *A Plain Account,* 86.

Chapter 9

1. *Philia* (the love of friendship), *storgē* (natural affection), *erōs* (the love of desire, self-seeking love), and *agapē* (in prebiblical Greek the love that "prefers" or "esteems" one person [or thing] more highly than another; in the New Testament, self-giving, redemptive love).

2. The classic treatment of these two motifs is Anders Nygren's *Agape and Eros* (Philadelphia: Muhlenberg Press, 1953).

3. A Greek myth is a poetic way of expressing a truth that defies rational or scientific explication.

4. *Erōs* does not occur in the New Testament, probably because of its orgiastic associations.

5. Genesis tells us that God formed Eve from one of the man's *ribs.* He did not form her from a bone of his foot, said the rabbis—Adam was not to trample on Eve. Nor did He form her from a bone of Adam's head—Eve was not to rule over the man. Rather, He formed her from

Adam's ribs—that Adam might love, shield, and protect her as his equal.

6. According to Genesis, marriage has a double purpose: for the procreation of the race (1:27-28), but also for personal fulfillment (2:18-24).

7. *The Confessions of St. Augustine,* trans. Edward B. Pusey (New York: Random House, 1949), 3. Pascal observed that there is "a God-shaped vacuum" in every human soul.

8. In the Greek of Christ's time, *agapē* was a colorless and rather uncommon term that the Church picked up and into which it poured the riches of the gospel (see William M. Greathouse, "Agapē," in *Beacon Dictionary of Theology,* ed. Richard S. Taylor [Kansas City: Beacon Hill Press of Kansas City, 1983], 31-32).

9. William Barclay, *The Letters of John and Jude,* rev. ed., in *Daily Study Bible Series* (Philadelphia: Westminster Press, 1976), 98.

10. Wesley, *Explanatory Notes upon the New Testament,* 915. For Wesley's classification of "babes" and "fathers," see 1 John 2:12-18 (*Notes,* 906-8).

11. Heitzenrater, *Wesley and the Methodists,* 308.

12. Barclay, *The Letters of John and Jude,* 98.

13. Robert T. Young, *A Sprig of Hope* (Nashville: Abingdon Press, 1980), 79.

Chapter 10

1. E. Stanley Jones, *Abundant Living* (New York: Abingdon Press, 1941), 157.

2. François Fénelon, *Christian Perfection,* ed. Charles F. Whiston, trans. Mildred Whitney Stillman (New York: Harper and Brothers Publishers, 1947), 36.

3. John Wesley asks: "Is this death to sin, and renewal in love, gradual or instantaneous?" Answer: "A man may be dying for some time; yet he does not, properly speaking, die, till the soul is separated from the body; and in that instant, he lives the life of eternity. In like manner, he may be dying to sin for some time; yet he is not dead to sin, till sin is separated from his soul; and in that instant, he lives the full life of love. . . . It is often difficult to perceive the instant when a man dies; yet there is an instant in which life ceases" (*A Plain Account,* 62, 115).

4. Oswald Chambers, *My Utmost for His Highest,* ed. James Reimann (Grand Rapids: Discovery House, 1992), Dec. 3.

5. Adam Clarke, *The New Testament of our Lord and Saviour Jesus Christ* (New York: Methodist Book Concern, n.d.), 1:639.

6. George A. Buttrick, *The Interpreter's Bible* (New York and Nashville: Abingdon Cokesbury Press, 1951), 7:266.

7. William M. Greathouse, *The Fullness of the Spirit* (Kansas City: Nazarene Publishing House, 1958), 89.

8. Stephen J. Harper, "The Devotional Life of John Wesley, 1703-1738" (Ph.D. diss., Duke University, 1981), 2:538.

9. This entire section, "How to Receive Sanctifying Grace," is extracted from Wesley D. Tracy et al., *The Upward Call: Spiritual Formation and the Holy Life* (Kansas City: Beacon Hill Press of Kansas City, 1994), 45-47.

Chapter 11

1. Wesley, "The Scripture Way of Salvation," 2:457-59.

2. George A. Mather and Larry A. Nichols, *Dictionary of Cults, Sects, Religions, and the Occult* (Grand Rapids: Zondervan Publishing House, 1993), 120.

3. Stephen M. Miller, ed., *Misguiding Lights?* (Kansas City: Beacon Hill Press of Kansas City, 1991), 61.

Chapter 12

1. John Leinenweber, *Love One Another, My Friends: St. Augustine's Homilies on the First Letter of John, an Abridged English Version* (San Francisco: Harper and Row, 1989), 83.

2. Bonnie Bowman Thurston, "Matthew 5:43-48," *Interpretation* 41 (April 1987): 173.

3. Wesley, *A Plain Account*, 99.

4. John Wesley, "The Way of the Kingdom," in *John Wesley's Sermons: An Anthology*, ed. Albert C. Outler and Richard P. Heitzenrater (Nashville: Abingdon Press, 1991), 127.